KINGDOM
BLUEPRINT

KINGDOM
BLUEPRINT

Cultivating an Intimate Relationship with God

Theressa Dawn Bremer McMorris, LMFT

MEDIA.COM

KINGDOM
BLUEPRINT

Published by
Illumify Media Global
IllumifyMedia.com
"Let's Bring Your Book to Life!"

Library of Congress Control Number: 2022908857

Paperback ISBN: 978-1-955043-71-7

Typeset by Art Innovations (http://artinnovations.in/)
Cover design by Debbie Lewis

Printed in the United States of America

To my God, who has loved me from the beginning: thank you.
To John, the man who always knew and believed
long before I did: thank you.
To Beth Fletcher Brokaw, my hero: thank you for being "skin on."
To Jack, Nick, and Sarah, my treasures: thank you.

The question forever asked is "Why?"
The answer is. . .
reverberating in our collective knowing
crying out from our birth
knowing at our death,
ringing in eternity
singing from creation
echoing in our hearts
whispering in the darkness
and celebrating in the light. . .

The answer is "Relationship."

CONTENTS

Introduction   xi

Chapter 1: The Question and the Answer   1
    Are Flashy Miracles the Answer?   2
    The Kingdom Blueprint   5

Chapter 2: The Kingdom Is . . .   8
    1. The Kingdom is Here   8
    2. The Kingdom is Now   9
    3. The Kingdom is Yada   13
    4. The Kingdom is Relationship. . .   15
    5. Born out of Relationship   16
    6. By Way of Relationship   18
    7. For Purposes of Relationship   19
    The Kingdom and The King   20
    God is and We are Relationship   21

Chapter 3: The Invitation: From God to Man   25
    The Interconnectedness of the World Around Us 26
    The Intimacy and Connectedness of Marriage   27
    The Intimacy and Connectedness of Sex   28
    The Intimacy and Connectedness of Raising Children 30
    The Interactive Nature of His Living Word   31
    At the Heart of His Relentless Pursuit is Relationship 32

Chapter 4: What keeps us from shouting "Yes!"?   34
    The Absence of Acceptance   35
    Hardening the Heart   36
    The Craving for Signs   37
    Filtering the Invitation through a Distorted Self 39

Chapter 5: Jesus' Response to Our Distorted and False Selves   44
    Gentle As We Go   44
    The Forming of the Self   45
    The False Self: The Illusion   48

Chapter 6: God Invites Us into Our True Selves   57
    Before the Whisper   58
    Who God Is Defines Who We Are   59
    His Power: Good   61
    Shared Life: Intimacy   63
    Love: An Invitation to Make Dinner   65

Chapter 7: His Presence Changes Everything   67
    Some Guiding Principles to Practicing the Presence   69
    Engaging with God's Presence   75

Chapter 8: The Transformative Power of Spiritual Disciplines   88
    Christian Spiritual Formation   90
    A Mind Set On   91
    Rehabilitation of the Flesh   92
    Shaking Loose and Moving Inward   93

Chapter 9: The Seven Disciplines   96
    The Three S's: Silence, Solitude, and Stillness   96
    Submission   102
    Confession   107
    Prayer   108
    Service   111
    Making it Personal   114

Chapter 10: Commission   118
    Commission: Relationship with One Another   118

Appendix: Characteristics of the False, Distorted, and True Self   134
Reference List   135
About the Author   137

A little over a decade ago, I was asked to speak on the seemingly simple topic of relationship for a church's annual meeting.

I am a systemic relational therapist, a Licensed Marriage and Family Therapist (LMFT). Most folks think our training only applies to marriages and families, but LMFTs are actually trained in systems, how parts of a system are in relationship with other parts of the system, and the dynamics inherent in all systems.

It certainly does have application in marriages and families. It also has application for all systems: churches, organizations, clubs, individuals, and even God. In fact, God is the perfect system; He is perfect relationship. This perfect God, this perfect system, this perfect relationship has created people that reflect Him. Collectively, they are known as His people, organized, as Dallas Willard puts it, under "his effectual reign"—His kingdom.

During the church annual meeting at which I spoke, when I was two-and-a-half hours into this three-hour seminar, a prominent pastor in the church raised his hand and said, "Yes, we know all this. Tell us what we don't know."

What this interruption crystallized for me is this reality: We may have the knowledge, but we do not *know* it.

There is a well-known quote credited to Papua New Guinea's Asaro Tribe: "Knowledge is only rumor until it lives in the bones." We do not know well how to be in nor how to sustain relationship with God, self, or one another. Just like the gentleman in that seminar, we nod our heads in affirmation, but our hearts are bleeding because we do not really know. We are lost, because we have lost the knowledge of how to be in relationship with God in such a way that our lives are dramatically transformed—so dramatically transformed that the world sees Jesus in us, and our presence with others illumines the Spirit of God and draws them to the eternal life they see in us.

We believe going to church, praying regularly, reading our Bible, and doing our devotionals are evidence of a relationship with God. That alone does not make a relationship. We have evidence to prove that. Similarly, sharing a bed, raising children, and saying "I do" does not make a marriage. We have evidence to prove that as well. Activity does not make a relationship.

> "Not everyone who says to Me, 'Lord, Lord,' will enter the kingdom of heaven, but he who does the will of My Father who is in heaven *will enter*. Many will say to Me on that day, 'Lord, Lord, did we not prophesy in Your name, and in Your name cast out demons, and in Your name perform many miracles?' And then I will declare to them, 'I never knew you; DEPART FROM ME, YOU WHO PRACTICE LAWLESSNESS.'"
> **Matthew 7:21–23**

This book takes a deep dive into what it looks like to be called into relationship with the Living God—and how to let Him transform our relationship with ourselves and one another, too.

In the following chapters, I explore the following:
- How to participate in the Kingdom of God now
- How relationship with God, self, and one another is the core blueprint of kingdom life, expansion, and transformation
- How to see and respond to God's relentless pursuit of us
- How to understand our defensiveness and avoidance (false self and distorted self) of this invitation

- How to discover our unique design (true self) for the kingdom now
- How to engage God's presence and be forever changed
- How your transformation is designed to engage the world
- How to engage the building of the kingdom now

We do not lack access to knowledge in our modern world. We have more translations of the Bible than we can count. What we need are lives transformed, beaconing out the light of God to the world. We need transformed lives that cause the world to stop in its tracks and wonder: Why are you so different? Why are you at peace? Why are you so kind and generous? Why are you filled with joy? This is how Christianity changed Rome. This is our Rome, and it is in desperate need of light!

CHAPTER 1

The Question and the Answer

Beneath life's daily questions like "What's for dinner?" "Where are we going on vacation?" or "Which side of the family are we spending Christmas with this year?", deeper questions haunt us. We may dismiss them, joke about them, or create bumper stickers for them, but still they linger.

- Why are we here?
- Why do I feel so alone?
- Why is there such a high divorce rate?
- Why is my marriage suffering?
- Where is the joy of my faith?
- We have complex questions with seemingly no answers.

Why are we working so hard for a promotion that will take us away from our family, the very people the promotion is intended to help? Why do we bother getting married when there is such a disturbingly high divorce rate? Why are so many children growing up without fathers? Why are our churches, which are supposed to be the missional outreach of Christ, so troubled?

Sometimes we hope the answers will be found in some future chapter of the book of our life:

- When I have a baby, I will be happy.
- When I get that promotion and the accompanying raise, I will be able to be at peace.
- When I join that gym and get that perfect body, I will finally like myself.
- When I finally have a nice house, our family will be happy.
- When my kids get into the best schools and are in the best athletic programs, they will be happy, and I will be a good mom.

Unfortunately, the answers to our questions on this whirling orb we call home are not typically found in the next chapter. They are not solved by the passing of time, the acquisition of things, or the amassing of power.

Much like drinking salt water, these things only create further thirst and emptiness.

Sometimes we cry out for miracles. We pray that our marriage will be miraculously healed. We pray our teen will stop taking drugs. We pray our friend will be healed from cancer. We pray for more money. We pray that our depression lifts. We seek divine intervention.

ARE FLASHY MIRACLES THE ANSWER?

Miracles are flashy. We like flashy. We love to share flashy, experience flashy, and do flashy. While the Kingdom of God can certainly have flashy moments, the preponderance of kingdom activity is not flashy but the tedious work of the small.

We love the story of the Red Sea but not so much the forty years of eating manna and walking in a desert.

We love the story of the flood, but not so much the 120 years of back–breaking ark–building work with the accompanying harassment, ridicule, and attacks.

The quiet and powerful work of the kingdom does not grab us. Jesus did flashy, and that certainly was what people wanted. But His real work of building the kingdom took place through loving relationships with people.

Jesus formed bonds with many people as He sojourned. In particular, scripture identifies His relationships with twelve very challenging men. While the transformation of this ragamuffin team was indeed a miracle, it was in no way flashy. Walking the dirt roads with no place to lay His head was not flashy (Luke 9:58). The cross was not flashy, yet that is where He went, and we are called to do the same (Matthew 16:24). And as we follow Him there, we are promised that we will never be alone, and herein lies the true miracle and purpose of the kingdom—relationship.

I am not calling for a revival of flashy miracles. I am calling for a revival of the miracle of relationship. I am calling for a revival of the miracle of the turning heart, a burning heart for God and those He loves. As the prophet writes in Malachi 4:6 (BSB), "He will turn the hearts of the fathers to their children, and the hearts of the children to their fathers. Otherwise, I will come and strike the land with a curse."

I am calling for a revival of the miracle of reconciliation.

> So from now on we regard no one from a worldly point of view. Though we once regarded Christ in this way, we do so no longer. Therefore, if anyone is in Christ, the new creation has come: The old has gone, the new is here! All this is from God, who reconciled us to Himself through Christ and gave us the ministry of reconciliation.
> **2 Corinthians 5:16–18 (NIV)**

I am calling for a revival of the miracle of grace distribution, as did Paul when he wrote in 1 Corinthians 13:6–7 (NLT), "It does not rejoice about injustice but rejoices whenever the truth wins out. Love never gives up, never loses faith, is always hopeful, and endures through every circumstance."

I am calling for the miracle of confession, as we read in James 5:16 (NIV): "Therefore confess your sins to each other and pray for each other so that you may be healed. The prayer of a righteous person is powerful and effective."

These are not six o'clock newsworthy miracles, but they are kingdom newsworthy miracles. These miracles occur when. . .

. . . a person is allowed to share her deepest pain with a listening loving ear.

. . . a person is safe enough to speak the deep, dark fears of how he feels about himself, God, and others.

. . . a person is free to speak of the bondage that has held him captive his entire life.

. . . a husband and wife for the first time are honest about their pain and fear and begin to understand each other and can begin to love again.

. . . a person of faith for the first time faces her fear and can truly begin to understand that God not only loves her but has a plan for her.

. . . one sister holds another sister through the grief of a regretted abortion that she will never be able to tell anyone else about.

These are miracles that bring darkness into the light. We are invited to walk into the darkness of others' worlds with the light of grace, the message of forgiveness, and the gift of eternal life hope. I am calling for a revival in the church to get back to what Christ called us to—relationship with God, self, and one another. Relationship is the reason this earth was created. Relationship is the reason Christ came. Relationship is the reason He died. Relationship is the reason He will come again.

The Kingdom of God on earth was born out of relationship, by way of relationship, for purpose of relationship.

THE KINGDOM BLUEPRINT

If the miracle of relationship is the answer to all of life's questions, how do we embrace this answer in our own lives? How do we share it with others?

Three processes fuel and further the kingdom, and they are all fueled by relationship. The three processes are Invitation, Transformation, and Commission. They are a self-replicating system, and they are the way of the kingdom.

1. **The invitation:** God beckons us. We either accept or reject that invitation.

2. **Our transformation:** As we interact with God—and with other people—we are transformed. Other people play a role in our transformation because there is a reciprocal process of how we influence the world and the world influences us—but it's not going to change the light of God in us. In fact, our interactions with the world actually help us become stronger.

3. **Our commission:** The truth is that we can't spend time in God's presence and not be transformed. And we are transformed, as we become more like Jesus, which reflects out to the world. In addition to reflecting who Jesus is to those around us, we also feel compelled to point others to God by way of relationship. This process of pointing others to God, or commission, comes in as many forms as there are people. When this sharing correlates with God's invitation, the process begins again.

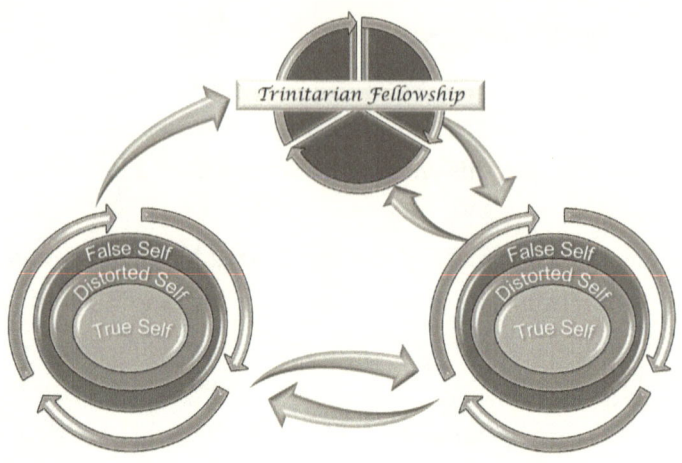

Let's look at how this process is revealed to us through the ministry of Jesus:

Jesus extended the invitation to twelve men. (There were so many others.) They were transformed through meaningful relationship and the embodiment of the Holy Spirit. This compelled them forward.

This is the nature of this process; it is compelling. Peter and John said it succinctly when the council warned them to not speak or teach in the name of Jesus in Acts 4:19–20: "Whether it is right in the sight of God to give heed to you rather than to God, you be the judge; for we cannot stop speaking about what we have seen and heard."

We see this process when folks are compelled into all forms of ministry. Sometimes it might not make much logical sense, but the person "has to" do it. It didn't make sense when Jesus did it, either. His family seemed to think He was crazy. With little to His name, Jesus invited some scruffy fisherman and a bunch of disenfranchised women into relationship, and He built His church.

Christendom has been guilty of viewing great preachers, televangelists, missionaries, big organizations, and bestselling Christian authors as the people responsible for fulfilling the great commission.

But this simply isn't true. It does not primarily fall on those who have been called to a pulpit or platform or foreign lands to fulfill the great commission.

This mission is for each and every person who hears the call of our Lord to follow Him. "Go into the world" means to engage. What does this look like? Right now, I am sitting in Denny's in East Syracuse, New York. This is "the world"—so I regularly engage with some waitresses and develop relationships. I really only had to go about three miles.

"God's future is among the regular, ordinary people of God. It's not primarily in great leaders or experts, but among the people, all those people most leaders believe don't get it" (Roxburgh and Romanuk, *The Missional Leader*, p. 21).

I would love to tell you that God has revealed to me brand new deep mysteries. Instead, I am a fellow traveler writing to you about truths that were understood for generations before us, but which seem to have been lost in our quick gimmicky *gotta–get–'em–saved*, slogan–driven, bumper–sticker convicting, drive–thru life.

God has a plan. He showed us how to do it. We have forgotten. We have lost our way.

> It is a tragic error to think that Jesus was telling us, as He left, to start churches, as that is understood today. From time to time, starting a church may be appropriate. But His aim for us is much greater than that. He wants us to establish "beachheads" or bases of operation for the Kingdom of God wherever you are. (Willard, *The Great Omission*, 2006)

This is the blueprint.

Now let's take a deeper look at what it means in our lives today.

CHAPTER 2

The Kingdom Is . . .

*The Kingdom of God on earth was born out of relationship, by
way of relationship, for purpose of relationship.*

The Sovereign is seated. All authority in heaven and on earth has
been given Him (Matthew 28:18). To live in the Kingdom of God
is to choose to live under the authority and governance of God,
the law of the universe. Under this King's reign, we love our neighbor as
we love our self. In this reality, we turn the other cheek. In this country,
we live by way of grace. It is here that violence is met with peace. In this
community, the good guy doesn't mind finishing last because that means
his neighbor finishes first. This is where we share our bread and don't
take it from another.

This kingdom is the Trinitarian relationship extended to mankind.
No one is forced into this kingdom, and all are wanted (2 Peter 3:9).

Here are seven frequently overlooked truths about the kingdom:

1. The Kingdom is Here

God's kingdom isn't a far–off place where fat baby–like angels sing
with harps as they float on the clouds, nor is it merely a passive residence

of those who have "said the prayer." The kingdom is here; it is now. Isn't that what He told us nearly two thousand years ago when He said, "The time is fulfilled, and the Kingdom of God is at hand; repent and believe in the gospel" (Mark 1:15).

He said it in so many different ways to so many different people. Didn't He give the kingdom invitation when He said, "Rise and walk" (Matthew 9:5 ESB)? Didn't He give the kingdom invitation when He said, "Your sins are forgiven" (Luke 7:48)? Didn't he give the kingdom invitation when He said, "Go and sin no more" (John 8:11 NLT)?

These all sound like invitations to me. He gave the invitation by meaningfully moving into people's lives, by way of relationship. Some took Him up on it and some walked away. But an offer was extended either way. He engaged with the person in front of Him and He gave what He had—his presence and the illumination of the kingdom, now.

For those who choose this kingdom reality, each step and redemptive misstep is a kingdom footprint. When Peter stepped out of the boat and began walking on water, he was walking in kingdom reality, fully engaged in relationship with Jesus, the King. When Paul lost his sight, he engaged with Jesus and gained kingdom sight. Facing death by rocks, Stephen gazed into Heaven and was fully alive in the glory of the kingdom. "The Kingdom of God is at hand" is what He said (Mark 1:15 ESV).

2. THE KINGDOM IS NOW

Yesterday and tomorrow are narratives carved out by perception and expectations. These narratives are, at best, distorted and often delusional. Most of our waking consciousness and energy are fueled by fear. We worry about the past and fear for the future.

The kingdom invitation is to leave this fear–fueled reality and enter a reality where we are perfectly safe right now, and tomorrow is provided for because He is our Sovereign.

For this reason I say to you, do not worry about your life, as to what you will eat; nor for your body, as to what you will put on . . . Consider the ravens, for they neither sow nor reap; they have no storeroom nor barn, and yet God feeds them; how much more valuable you are than the birds! And which of you by worrying can add a single hour to his life's span? . . . Consider the lilies, how they grow: they neither toil nor spin; but I tell you, not even Solomon in all his glory clothed himself like one of these. . . And do not seek what you will eat and what you will drink, and do not keep worrying. For all these things the nations of the world eagerly seek; but your Father knows that you need these things. But seek His kingdom, and these things will be added to you.
Luke 12:22–31

This reminds me of when my children were young and they were worried whether we would provide the right school supplies, the right shoes, the right Valentine's Day cards and candy, the right lunch snacks, or any other very serious concern. My response was a gentle invitation into the moment.

"Sweetie, don't we always get the things you need?" I would ask.

"Yes, Mommy," my children always answered.

The invitation was to remain in relationship with me and trust what they knew about me.

Similarly, if Jesus invites us not to worry about tomorrow, where might He be inviting us? Isn't the Kingdom of God at hand (Mark 1:15; Matthew 3:2; Matthew 10:7)? Might He be drawing us to the now? Seek first His kingdom and His righteousness? Might He be saying, "Do not worry, be with me; I am right here. I want to be with you while you clean the garage. I want to be with you as you drive in that congested traffic."

Might He be inviting us to cooperate with Him in what He is doing right now in the midst of what we are doing right now? Mirrored in the most common admonition found in scripture, our Lord invites us to be present with Him, here and now, for that is where He is working.

> Be strong and courageous, do not be afraid or tremble at them, for the LORD your God is the one who goes with you. He will not fail you or forsake you.
> **Deuteronomy 31:6**

> Do not fear! Stand by and see the salvation of the LORD which He will accomplish for you today.
> **Exodus 14:13**

> Be anxious for nothing, but in everything by prayer and supplication with thanksgiving let your requests be made known to God.
> **Philippians 4:6**

> But the LORD said to me, Do not fear him, for I have delivered him and all his people and his land into your hand; and you shall do to him just as you did to Sihon king of the Amorites, who lived at Heshbon.
> **Deuteronomy 3:2**

> Do not fear or be dismayed! Be strong and courageous, for thus the LORD will do to all your enemies with whom you fight.
> **Joshua 10:25**

> Peace I leave with you; My peace I give to you; not as the world gives do I give to you. Do not let your heart be troubled, nor let it be fearful.
> **John 14:27**

Then David said to his son Solomon, "Be strong and courageous, and act; do not fear nor be dismayed, for the LORD God, my God, is with you. He will not fail you nor forsake you until all the work for the service of the house of the LORD is finished.
1 Chronicles 28:20

In God, whose word I praise, In God I have put my trust; I shall not be afraid. What can *mere* man do to me?
Psalm 56:4

[Cast] all your anxiety on Him, because He cares for you.
1 Peter 5:7

Now is the invitation. Now is where the work of the kingdom is. Now is where you are invited to cooperate with Jesus. The kingdom is being built, one person at a time, one moment at a time. The invitation is to participate in the place you have been set, in the duties you have been given, in the territory you are to steward. He is doing it with you; He says He will never leave.

If you are busy doing the nine to five, then you are engaging in the work of provision for the kingdom territory you have been given. If you are washing dirty diapers, then you are engaging in the management of the territory you have been given, serving His creations. If you have small children, then you have been given the duty of portraying a loving parent to the most precious of His kingdom. The parental relationship is the foundation of our children's understanding of this invisible God. As parents, we truly are emissaries for the Most High God.

Your participation in the kingdom is now, where you have been placed and what you are to steward. It is all too human to believe the territory you have been given is too small and to want more. It is not a sin to want more, but it certainly can become one. Your call is to be here, right now.

What or who is in front of you? That is the work of the kingdom. Your God is the one who goes before and behind (Psalm 139:5). He has taken care of the past and is taking care of the future. If I can be so bold as to add the Oswald Chambers saying, "Trust God, do the next right thing, and release the outcomes."

The outcome is God's territory.

3. THE KINGDOM IS YADA

At the end of a very long day, I often ponder the vastness and commonness of all the pain I have seen that day and in the fullness of my career as a psychotherapist and my citizenship on this earth and in this kingdom.

I suppose on some level, I am wrestling with making sense of it all. These reflections made me understand that there is only ever one issue I work with. This issue can take many forms: abuse, loneliness, affairs, insecurity, addiction, anxiety, depression, communication issues, conflict, suicide, grief, anger, and more. And yet, the underlying problem is always the same: the anticipated or actual experience of abandonment and rejection.

In other words, broken relationship. At the core of all our pain is this singular reality, and it shapes everything we do. At our core, we were designed to be connected to God, our self, and one another.

Standing in defiant hope against this core pain is *yada*, the purpose of the kingdom: the restoration of relationship. *Yada* is the answer to what was broken so very long ago.

Yada is a rich Hebrew word encompassing the spectrum of meaningful relationship. In its fourth chronological appearance, the word *yada* is used to describe sexual intimacy among mankind, first experienced between Adam and Eve. "And Adam knew [*yada*] Eve his wife; and she conceived, and bare Cain, and said, I have gotten a man from the LORD" (Genesis 4:1 KJV).

Translated "knew," it is here that the word *yada* is used to describe the closest of human relationships—sexual union. The marital relationship is designed to be a place where you are fully known—good, bad, beautiful, ugly—and dearly loved still. *Yada* answers the deep agonizing fear of possible rejection and abandonment. *Yada* is the promise that relationship will never be broken, and you will be loved no matter what you have done (Romans 8:1). *Yada*, the hope of marriage, is an echo of the divine invitation of our Trinitarian God to be in relationship with you. *Yada* is at the heart of the kingdom. Deep meaningful relationship is at the heart of our God.

It is here that you can live in communion with God as your truest imperfect self, your fullest self. It is here that you stand in the land of eternal love: the most dangerous ground and safest place you will ever be. It is here that you are in the very hands of the Creator of the stars. It is here you are known.

> You who have been borne by Me from birth
> And have been carried from the womb;
> Even to your old age I will be the same,
> And even to your graying years I will bear you!
> I have done it, and I will carry you;
> And I will bear you and I will deliver you.
> **Isaiah 46:3–4**

It is here that your soul is beckoned home in order to heal the deep ache in your very substance, the desire to be deeply known and to deeply know.

> Deep calls to deep
> in the roar of your waterfalls;
> all your waves and breakers
> have swept over me.

By day the LORD directs his love,
at night his song is with me—
a prayer to the God of my life.
Psalm 42:7–8 (NIV)

This call of the deep to the deep is nearly irresistible—it is the long-ing call of the lover to the loved. This is Trinitarian Relationship, a place where deep knows deep—that place beyond words; the place that draws us. The invitation is to live in this kingdom reality. The invitation is to live in intimate Trinitarian relationship. This is the fulfillment of *yada*. This is the kingdom: born out of relationship, by way of relationship, for purpose of relationship.

4. THE KINGDOM IS RELATIONSHIP. . .

*The Kingdom of God on earth was born out of relationship, by
way of relationship, for purpose of relationship.*

Relationship is the fixed point of the kingdom. It is the reason. It is the method. It is the purpose. Every aspect of God's activity with, plan for, and context of mankind is organized by way of relationship. Nothing else really exists. But, alas, we fail to grasp the reality of what is right in front of us and all around. Our purpose is *not* to know the "most right" information. Our purpose is *not* to save lost souls—that is His job. Our purpose is *not* to have more seats in the pew. Our purpose is not to do great things for God.

The scariest words in the Bible reflect this truth when Jesus said, "Many will say to Me on that day, 'Lord, Lord, did we not proph-esy in Your name, and in Your name cast out demons, and in Your name perform many miracles?' And then I will declare to them, 'I never knew you; DEPART FROM ME, YOU WHO PRACTICE LAWLESSNESS'" (Matthew 7:22–23).

We have one purpose, and that is to glorify God. Any glorification
of God can only be a byproduct, a fruit of an outcome of relationship
with Him, ourselves, and one another. To glorify God is not to acknowledge God. The demons and the devil do that. The glory that He desires
is the fruit of a deeply forming intimate relationship, and it cannot be
done outside of relationship with Him, ourselves, and one another.

We cannot acknowledge, let alone glorify, Him if we are not in relationship with Him (Matthew 16:15–17). We cannot love Him if we do
not engage with ourselves and follow His commands (John 14:15). We
cannot love Him if we do not love one another (John 13:34–35). None
of these things can even be understood or attempted if we are not in relationship with Him, who is by His nature in relationship with Himself:
three distinct beings, one substance.

5. Born out of Relationship

Whether you believe the story of creation to be literal or metaphor-
ical makes no difference. This is the narrative given us to understand our
earthly beginnings.

> God spoke: "Let us make human beings in our image, make them
> reflecting our nature
> So they can be responsible for the fish in the sea,
> the birds in the air, the cattle,
> And, yes, Earth itself,
> and every animal that moves on the face of Earth."
> God created human beings;
> he created them godlike,
> Reflecting God's nature.
> He created them male and female.
> God blessed them:
> "Prosper! Reproduce! Fill Earth! Take charge!
> Be responsible for fish in the sea and birds in the air,

for every living thing that moves on the face of Earth."
Genesis 1:26–28 (MSG)

In this passage, the word *God* is translated from the word *'Elohi-ym*. 'Elohiym, a self-relational entity, God in community with Himself, creates mankind, which reflects His image. This one true God refers to Himself in both plural and singular. "God spoke" is singular. This singular one true God then self-references as "us," plural as well as singular. Deuteronomy 6:4 in one sentence declares this God that is in relationship with Himself. "Hear, O Israel! The LORD is our God, the LORD is one!"

> The LORD (Jehovah: the proper name of the one true God)
> *is our*
> God ('Elohiym: the plural version)

Again, singular representation goes hand in hand with plural representation. The phrase *in our image* is described by the Gesenius's Hebrew–Chaldee Lexicon as a "shadowing forth." While God's full nature is surely a mystery, our consideration of it here reveals an inherently relational God who created mankind as a shadowing forth of His relational self.

He created us to look like Him and then He created us out of the dust of the ground, which is part of an inherently relational system that screams His presence and reflects His relationship nature, much as children are born out of the relationship between one man and one woman. Relationship creates relationship; it is its nature, self-propelling and self-recreating. (I am quite confident a true theologian could come through this last paragraph and tear it apart. I am perfectly okay with that. I am just musing not defending a theological treatise.)

A wedding not yet paid off and a miraculous bump emerges, a creation, "made in our image. . . reflecting our nature"—little hims and hers. Even our personal kingdoms are born out the one relationship of two persons: "one flesh" (Mark 10:8).

I believe it is worthy of note that this relational God made humans to be in relationship with the rest of creation. "So they can" is a great phrase. So they can learn to rule, co–rule with Christ. We were always meant to be with God in relationship with God, managing our part of the world with Him.

The Kingdom of God on earth was born out of relationship, by way of relationship, for purpose of relationship.

6. BY WAY OF RELATIONSHIP

"My God, my God, why have you forsaken me?"

Bill paid, relationship purchased by way of relationship.

Divine Holy Relationship was handed over, much like we hand over cash in order to obtain a house, a car, or groceries. Jesus handed over his only currency—relationship with the Father. This is all He had, for he did not even have a place to lay His head (Luke 9:58). He gave up His intimate relationship with the Father in order that we might have unrestricted intimate relationship with the Holy Father. He opened the door to relationship with the Trinity by way of relationship. He gave us deep intimate personal relationship to the Living Almighty God. He gave us *yada*.

When a soul chooses relationship with Jesus Christ, the bill is stamped paid, and a home is purchased in the Holy Kingdom of God. House by house, person by person, relationship by relationship, He is building a kingdom.

"Do you not know that you are a temple of God and that the Spirit of God dwells in you? If anyone destroys the temple of God, God will destroy that person; for the temple of God is holy, and that is what you are (1 Corinthians 3:16–17).

The kingdom cannot be built with gold and silver, as Peter demonstrates when he says, "Silver and gold I do not have, but what I do have I give you: In the name of Jesus Christ of Nazareth, rise up and walk" (Acts 3:6 NKJV). Peter gave what he had; he had a relationship with Jesus Christ. Jesus gave what He had; He had a relationship with the Father. He would soon provide a relationship with the Holy Spirit. From that relationship, a home was purchased for the kingdom.

While correct doctrine and right understanding is critically important, it is not an assent to truth that saved the thief on the cross, the woman at the well, the woman caught in adultery, the little man in the tree, or any of the disciples; it was a yielding to relationship, a living, dynamic, intimate relationship. Relationship is what He had; it is what He did. Jesus loved the person in front of Him. One temple at a time was and is purchased by way of relationship. He engaged in relationship whomever crossed His path, whether in a tree or by way of a tug on His robe. The kingdom revolves around the greatest commandment: "You shall love the Lord your God with all your heart, and with all your soul, and with all your mind. And the second is like unto it, You shall love your neighbor as yourself. . . "—relationship.

The Kingdom of God on earth was born out of relationship, by way of relationship, for purpose of relationship.

7. For Purposes of Relationship

"The aim of God in history is the creation of an all–inclusive community of loving persons, with Himself included in that community as its prime sustainer and most glorious inhabitant." –Dallas Willard

God is creating a community of folks who want to be in relationship with Him. There are many names for this community: the Church, the Way, believers, the great cloud of witnesses, the saints, the faithful and the Kingdom of God. It is in the midst of this community that He resides, for this is the purpose of His kingdom, "that they may all be one; even as You, Father, are in Me and I in You, that they also may be in Us" (John 17:21). It is this intimacy that unifies the body, binding us one to another, for the great mystery is that this community is His body (Ephesians 5:30; Colossians 1:4). It is out of this intimacy with God that we cannot but glorify Him. For when you see Him, He is truly glorious.

From the moment of conception (created out of relationship) to the end of our earthly days (and I would suggest that relationship survives us in others), we experience, create, build, seek, work on, recover, harm, break, get frustrated with, and grieve the loss of relationships.

In fact, we are constantly creating relationships: school yard besties, girlfriends and boyfriends passing notes in class, girls' nights out, bands of brothers, college fraternities, political parties, coworkers, college classmates, block parties, high school reunions, unions, mobs and gangs, churches, PTA. The list is endless. It is what we are wired to do.

THE KINGDOM AND THE KING

History chronicles rulers who have used their power to serve and rulers who have used their power to extort. Their kingdoms have either thrived or suffered. The nature of a king or queen, as case would have it, will inevitably be reflected in the nature of His kingdom.

The Kingdom of God is, likewise, a reflection of the nature of God. The Trinity, in its very mysterious nature, is relationship: three persons, one being: perfect relationship seeking relationship.

"God in His Trinity of subsistent relations infinitely transcends every shadow of selfishness. For the One God does not subsist apart and alone in His Nature; He subsists as Father and as Son and as Holy Ghost. These Three Persons are one, but apart from them God does not subsist also as One. He is not Three Persons plus one nature, therefore four! He is Three Persons, but One God. He is at once infinite solitude (one

nature) and perfect society (Three Persons). One Infinite Love
in three subsistent relations."
–**Thomas Merton,** *New Seeds of Contemplation*

Relationship, by definition, refers to a state of being. This is God's
eternal state. His nature is relationship. This aspect of His nature exists
simultaneously in fullness with all of His other qualities. He is holy. He
is righteous. He is just. He is love. He is good. He is light. He is invisible.
He is relationship.

GOD IS AND WE ARE RELATIONSHIP

For some, it might be a bold statement to say that our Trinitarian
God is relationship. It would be far easier to say that God is simply relational. He is, of course, that. However, being relational is not a state of
being, it is the action produced from the state. To say that God is only
relational is to minimize His state of being to an action. The Trinity is
relationship; this is His state of being.

I am Mom. It's not an action. It's not a label. It's a state of being. Being a mom by label only doesn't produce parental behavior—but
when it is a state of being, it does. At my core, as a mom my nature is
relationship. From the moment my son was conceived, at my core, I
became Mom. My nature changed, and it can never change back. (This
is why when people casually dismiss a miscarriage, it can be hurtful to
a mom and dad. Conception/adoption changes a soul, much like being
"born again" changes a soul. It changes the state of being.) To say that I
am relational with my son doesn't come close to articulating the very essence of who I am. Being relational is an action that begins and ends. My
son and I are tied forever as mother and son. We are knit at our hearts.
He is my flesh. He is a part of my soul. We belong to one another. We
are bound. He will one day marry another and be knit to her, but he will
never cease being my son. At my core, as a mom, I am not relational; I
am relationship.

To talk about relationship in this way is difficult for a variety of reasons. We tend to think of relationship, in our common and degraded use of the word, as something we move in and out of. We use the word like we use the word *party* or *home*, something to engage or dispense. I am at a party; I am in a relationship. I left my home; I left my relationship. We do not understand that relationship is our permanent state; it is our nature; we cannot disengage. Once in a relationship with someone, it never ends. You may cease to talk to that person or see that person, but that person becomes a part of you. Relationship is permanent, despite what we do with it.

In our culture we do not perceive relationship as it is: eternal, unbreakable, an attribute of our existence. In our culture (and all cultures to one degree or another) we engage with the concept of relationship casually and simplistically. We minimize it, toss it around, and behave as if we can carelessly discard it. Casual engagement with intimate relationships not only corrodes the core of who we are, it propagates the lie that we are merely highly evolved animals.

The truth is that we are so much more. The truth is that we are sons and daughters of the Most High God, made in His image, bearing his likeness. The truth is that relationship is an attribute of who He is and who we are.

From birth to death and beyond, this is our being. Not a moment can be separated from this reality. Relationship with God, self, and one another is all there is. It may sound extreme, but the truth is that we are part of one another. I am connected to you and you are connected to me. As I am careless with my life, I hurt you. As you engage or don't engage with God, you change my life. As you touch my life, my life with God is changed. These are interchangeable, inextricable realities.

The interconnectedness/oneness/undividedness of God, self, and one another cannot be broken. This is not a new version of pantheism or panentheism. This is not universalism nor is it any other "ism" at all. It is the mystery of marriage, the Trinity, and relationship. The Trinity is three but one. Marriage is two but one. We will stand alone before the throne of God, but Jesus stands for us. Paul said it as well as it can be said when he wrote, "For just as each of us has one body with many members, and these members do not all have the same function, so in Christ we, though many, form one body, and each member belongs to all the others (Romans 12: 4-5 NIV). We are one body, the body of Christ. We are one part of the body, and it cannot stand alone. We belong to one another in Christ.

When I was younger, I puzzled over Jesus' instructions to leave our gifts at the altar, go reconcile with our brothers, then come and offer our sacrifices (Matthew 5:24). Shouldn't we reconcile with God first? Shouldn't we worship Him first?

Equally puzzling are His words that if we feed, clothe, and visit the "least of them," we have done this to Him. Jesus also said that, with the giving of the Holy Spirit, if we forgive anyone's sins, they will be forgiven but if we don't, they won't (John 20:22–23). And why does He say that we must forgive others so we can be forgiven (Mark 11:25)? Or that confessing my sins to another person can heal me (James 5:16)?

I can take these words at face value, or I can look deeper and find that in this kingdom, God, self, and one another are interdependent and cannot be separated. I will confess that aspects of the above remain a mystery for me. I do not fully understand, but what I do understand is that somehow, we are all a part of one another and what we do among ourselves impacts heaven and heaven has promised to respond.

Rugged individualism in America has run amok. Individualism that destroys others isn't individualism; it's abuse. America's great strength has become a great weakness.

While it's true that oppression results when community denies individuality, it is equally true that when individualism stands apart from community, it becomes narcissism. Healthy individualism can only be healthy if it is responsible to community and vice versa. I am responsible for me and responsible to you (community) is the phrase that helps discern the balance. (Attachment and differentiation are the words we use in the psychological community for this balance.) When we disregard this balance, we wreak havoc.

We are eternal beings interacting with other eternal beings. Yet, we treat each other, ourselves, and God as if we are yesterday's newspaper or last hour's news headline. It is a horrifying reality. We are eternal beings and our actions toward each other have eternal implications. When one witnesses the bewildering inability of a person to extricate themselves from the nightmare of an emotionally and/or physically violent relationship, we see how we are inextricably part of one another (in the case of abuse, disorderedly part of one another). Watching a child turn back in desperate hopes of being loved by the parent who has just beaten them, we see the undeniable core of our nature: relationship. We are bound to one another. We are not relational to one another. We are and God is relationship.

Relationship is the only thing we have, and it is the only thing that will change us. Outside of a glorified body, which I might suggest is the story keeper of all of our relationships, there is nothing else we have that survives this earthly existence except relationship to God, self, and one another. There are some who know Him and may even do great things in his name, but the defining factor is whether they are in relationship with the Father (Matthew 7:21–23). Relationship is all there is. Everything else is an illusion.

"To live spiritually in the world is to unmask the illusion, dispel the darkness, and walk in the light."
–Henri Nouwen

CHAPTER 3

The Invitation: From God to Man

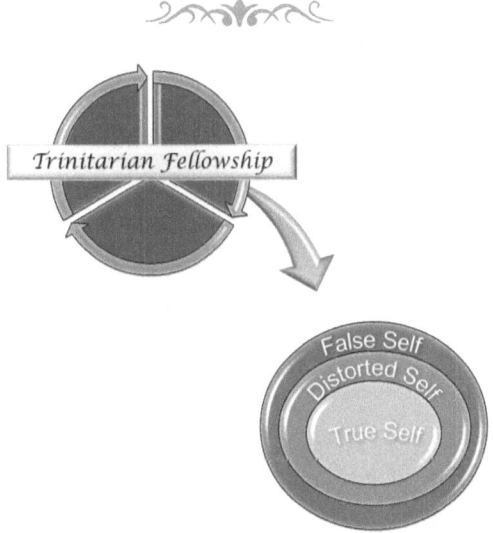

How do we recognize God's invitation to us? How do we even know that He exists, much less that He is inviting us into relationship with Himself?

Acts of creation including architecture, art, books, and even sidewalk art cast shadows of the creator. Even the simple creation of a pot of soup can shadow forth the soul-love of a mom for her family.

'Elohiym, the Creator, is casting His shadow.

Will we see him?

The truth is, how can we not? All of creation silently screams who he is. When we think about the relational makeup of the physical world in which we live, God is revealed. In the intimacies of marriage, sex, and raising children, we see His heart. In the interactive nature of His living Word, we find Him.

Let's take a deeper look at each of these. And as we do, His invitation to us becomes undeniable.

THE INTERCONNECTEDNESS OF THE WORLD AROUND US

"Every detail of the creative order only magnifies the extraordinary integration of all things. Simply put, the unifying principle of the Universe is relationship."
–Erwin Raphael McManus

'Elohiym created a universe and plopped a blue whirling orb of explosive interconnected relationship somewhere in the middle of it. What does this orb tell us about the creator?

Now the earth was formless and empty, darkness was over the surface of the deep, and the Spirit of God was hovering over the waters. And God said, "Let there be light," and there was light.
Genesis 1:2–3 (NIV)

There is light and dark. The two, while seemingly in conflict, reveal a surprising union. Light happens and then dark happens and then light—an intimate dance of eloquence and beauty, rest and work. The first act of creation is an interdependent relationship between dark and light.

Then water and sky and water and land. The land's thirsty so the sky helps out and pulls the water up and moves it around and back into land, where the land releases the water back to itself. More dynamic unfolding. . .

Then God said, "Let the land produce vegetation: seed–bearing plants and trees on the land that bear fruit with seed in it, according to their various kinds." And it was so. The land produced vegetation: plants bearing seed according to their kinds and trees bearing fruit with seed in it according to their kinds.

Genesis 1:11–12 (NIV)

Vegetation is the bounty of land, sky, and sun moving seamlessly as partners—deeply connected and relational. This explosion of vegetation makes provision for His finest creation. 'Elohiym brings forth man—both male and female. This creation then is invited to dance, one of our favorite activities, which brings forth more little "hims" and "hers." 'Elohiym has shown us who He is. The earth and all that is in it is a reflection of His relationship nature. He syncs it all together. 'Elohiym, man, earth, animals, vegetation—let the whole of the creation relationship dance.

THE INTIMACY AND CONNECTEDNESS OF MARRIAGE

Marriage, a most sacred of bindings, is a shadow, a reflection, of the unknowable Holy Trinitarian Fellowship. It is in the marriage crucible that we are forged into the image of God. Marriage, one of the hardest endeavors we will ever undertake, is the place where we get a glimpse of the oneness of God. Marriage is where we come to the hard understanding that love is not a feeling but a choice. Love is the hard path of "for better or worse." There is a reason that many marriage ceremonies begin with "Marriage is not to be entered into lightly but reverently."

Marriage is intended to be a shadow reflection of the essence of our God, the perfect oneness of the Father, Son, and Holy Spirit. Marriage is an invitation to the practice of yielding one to another for the sake of the other. Christ, as always, is our guide. Christ yields to the needs of the church. He loved us first. He died for us. He intercedes for us. He says He will never leave us. Everything He did on this patch of dirt was for the church, yielding to the guidance of the Father and yielding to the movement of the Holy Spirit. As Paul said, "This mystery is great; but I am speaking with reference to Christ and the church" (Ephesians 5:32). Marriage is intended to be a reflection of God's love relationship with the church. This is discussed later in Chapter 6.

In Christendom, we know marriage is good and divorce is bad. But we don't know why marriage is good. We have some automated responses, but we don't know why it is good. I am not Catholic but the fact that marriage is a sacrament in that system makes me think that they are a little closer than we are.

There is much talk about how many divorces there are today. I tire of the discussion. We've been doing marriage poorly for a long time. Staying married for the sake of staying married while destroying one another does not please God. Staying married is not the issue. Understanding the high calling of marriage is more to the point.

Many of today's marriages are not marriages; they are impulsive and reactive couplings of folks who want to get their needs met and be "happy"—a great lie. If we get married to get our needs met, it likely will lead to ruin. If we enter marriage to truly love and serve the other, individual healing can and often does occur.

This is in the same vein that Christ says that if we are to lead, we must serve. True leadership is servanthood. True marriage is yielding to one another out of love and sacrifice. Yielding and sacrifice, if voluntary, is *not* abuse. Don't listen to that lie.

THE INTIMACY AND CONNECTEDNESS OF SEX

So the Lord God caused a deep sleep to fall upon the man, and he slept; then He took one of his ribs and closed up the flesh at that place.

The LORD God fashioned into a woman the rib which He had taken from the man, and brought her to the man. The man said,

"This is now bone of my bones,
And flesh of my flesh;
She shall be called Woman,
Because she was taken out of Man."

For this reason a man shall leave his father and his mother, and
be joined to his wife; and they shall become one flesh. And the
man and his wife were both naked and were not ashamed
Genesis 2:22–25

I wonder if Adam was able to articulate this ache inside him—this
aloneness. Would he know how to identify this need, or would he need
some help? Made for relationship and alone as the only human, animals were brought before him to name. Awareness of his human solitude
grew and produced a longing that prepared him to receive the greatest
of blessings. In this vacancy, this absence, this void, God was revealing
Himself through the yearnings of man, the yearning for relationship. As
it is today. So often, God must show us what we are missing before He
can give us the thing we need. Otherwise, we would not see it.

Sleep.

Eve!

"This is now bone of my bones and flesh of my flesh." This is the
cry known by all who have tasted intoxicating union. It is here, out of
a promise that we will never stray to another's bed, we can physically
experience and share the deepest parts of ourselves. It is here we are truly
known, loved, and safe. Almost Edenic, the marital bed is to be naked
and unashamed and free—to know another and be truly known by another—*yada*. The vacancy now satisfied—deeply intimately satisfied. A
union of two made one flesh. A gift given reflects another reality.

He is Three Persons, but One God. . . . One Infinite Love
in three subsistent relations. In the Father the infinite love

of God is always beginning; in the Son it is always full; and in the Holy Spirit it is perfect and it is renewed and never ceases to rest in its everlasting source. But if we follow Love forward and backward from Person to Person, we can never track it to a stop, we can never corner it and hold it down and fix it to one of the Persons, as if He could appropriate to Himself the fruit of the love of the others. For the One Love of the Three Persons is an infinitely rich giving of itself which never ends and is never taken, but is always perfectly given, only received in order to be perfectly shared. (Merton, *Seeds of Contemplation*, p. 68)

THE INTIMACY AND CONNECTEDNESS OF RAISING CHILDREN

I married this great guy, and we have this great amazing love. I wanted to recreate it. Did I say, "Let us make a child in our image"? No, that would be weird. Yet isn't that exactly what we said?

The truth is that we rarely find beautiful things and hide them. In fact, what we tend to do is recreate them. I have a beautiful Monet in my living room. It cost $50.

Three bundles of replication later, it is intimacy and bonding which was being replicated. Folks unable to have their own children speak commonly of a deep emptiness, an aching. Children provide an intimacy and a connectedness that is unique and cannot be found in adults, friends, mates, parents, siblings. I deeply love my husband. As husband and wife, we are connected in ways that pass our full understanding. In some ways, it is a different kind of love because we choose to love. We choose to be married.

But children are different. Yes, we choose to have children, but they are *our* children. There is an absolute—there is an unbreakable tie. There is a "from my body" kind of connection. Experiencing the weighty love for a child, I am disposed to understand God's love for me. I am disposed to think of the sacrifice of His body for us.

Because the creature itself also shall be delivered from the
bondage of corruption into the glorious liberty of the children
of God.
Romans 8:21 (KJV)

For ye are all the children of God by faith in Christ Jesus.
Galatians 3:26 (KJV)

Having predestinated us unto the adoption of children by
Jesus Christ to himself, according to the good pleasure of his
will.
Ephesians 1:5 (KJV)

Ye are of God, little children, and have overcome them: because
greater is he that is in you, than he that is in the world.
1 John 4:4 (KJV)

The relationships that God has given us are mere shadows of who
He is and what we are being invited into. These are not only reflections
of who He is, but they are enticements, invitations, requests, summons,
and provocations to come to Him. While what we have here on earth
in the form of family and marriage are good—really good—they are
but mere reflections of the deeper, the fuller, the *yada* relationship that
'Elohiym is and invites us into.

I do not pray for these alone, but also for those who will
believe in Me through their word; that they all may be one, as
You, Father, are in Me, and I in You; that they also may be one
in Us, that the world may believe that You sent Me.
John 17:20–21 (KJV)

The Interactive Nature of His Living Word

The Holy Word of God is Jesus Christ in ink and pulp. A phenomenon experienced through the generations for those who put themselves before it, the Word of God is life altering and cosmos shaking. Much like Moses meeting God on Mount Sinai and coming down with a glowing face, you cannot be truly in the presence of the Holy Word led by the Holy Spirit and not be changed. The living Word of God will comfort you, challenge you, heal you, invite you, convict you, love you, and change you if you yield to it. Otherwise, it is merely a piece of literature.

Despite all the convicting work of the Holy Spirit, we still have free will. But isn't that the point? We have free will. We have the free will to choose to humbly come before the Word of God and let it change us. If we do not, it will not. The Word of God is a petition for our presence, not a warrant for our arrest.

At the Heart of His Relentless Pursuit is Relationship

Graciously relentlessly pursuing the soul of man, this Hound of Heaven demands neither service nor performance. He extends the invitation to live in communion, to live in Trinitarian fellowship with the self-described God of Love, a love that surpasses understanding. "Nothing compares," cries the Apostle Paul. "Where else is there to go?" cries Peter. This invitation is extended as a gift. As a gift, it must always remain by its very nature free. The nature of a love relationship requires that both parties are free—both pursuer and pursued.

> We are entering into a living relationship that begins and develops in mutual freedom. God grants us perfect freedom because He desires creatures who freely choose to be in relationship with Him. . . Relationships of this kind can never be manipulated or forced. (Foster, *Prayer*, 1992)

Invitations are inherently laden with hope and tension. To answer the invitation is pregnant with fear and the hope of possibility. In the vacancy of an answer, we are drawn to the palpable unresolved tension. The inviter must await the answer because love is free.

Stripping away, for a moment, all the "correct" doctrine, all the historical theological violations, all liturgy, legalism, "ought" and "should" traditions, definitions of this and that, what do we find? The complexity of these matters can become disorienting, if they become the focus, the god.

As mentioned earlier, if we become so consumed with providing a good living for our family, we seek promotion after promotion, which inevitably takes us further away from family—has the point not been lost? So, asking again, if we strip all things of religious institution away for a moment, what do we find? We find a God who is relationship. His essence is relationship. He created this earth that is designed at its foundation on the concept of interconnected relationship. We find a God who created a soul for the sole purpose of relationship. We find a God beckoning, calling, inviting, offering relationship. Before the existence of earth, before a breath was even considered, He acted in love *first*.

From this position, where all things are stripped away, what might change as we exist in His reality, if we were driven by relationship and not doctrine? Might we begin to consider that maybe our "correct doctrine" has become an idol that communicates that "I'm righter than you," which at its nature breaks relationship? "Is man made for the Sabbath or the Sabbath made for man?" A good question, I think.

For His Divine Holy purpose, this God of relationship beckons us. He stands at the door and knocks. We are being invited into the fellowship of the Trinity. We are being invited to partake of an intimate community of *yada*. He stands at the door and knocks because we are free to choose. An answer—either in the affirmative, the negative, or the absence of an answer—is given. Do we choose to have a relationship with Him or without Him? In his book *Life with God*, Richard Foster eloquently articulates that the real question from God to man has always been, "I am with you. Will you be with me?"

CHAPTER 4

What keeps us from shouting "Yes!"?

R elationship with God. Quite the invitation!

So what keeps us from shouting "Yes!"? What obstacles do we face as we ponder the invitation of a lifetime? Of eternity?

Here are four of the most common obstacles we face.

THE ABSENCE OF ACCEPTANCE

Free will must have its place. To not respond to an invitation is to respond with a declination. Ignoring the petition doesn't make the reality of the invitation magically vanish.

Early on in our marriage, my husband taught me the great talent of not answering the phone just because it is ringing. I am grateful for the skill of not compulsively jumping to every ring. However, the reality is that there are matters that must be addressed. Not answering the phone call does not make the matter disappear.

Relationships take effort to maintain. Now, not all relationships need the same level of tending, but intimate caring relationships require pursuit, tending, and care. Much like my relationship with my house plants, they can only be ignored for so long. If we regularly and consistently say no and/or avoid invitations to be connected, relationships end or lose receptivity.

The offer has been given: "I am with you. Will you be with me?"

Deep in that place of knowing, when we turn away from the small conviction, the gentle nudge, we close our ears to the whisper of God. A consistent turning dulls the capacity to hear and limits the ability to turn.

As a counselor, I witness lives in the throes of consequences resulting from the choice to repeatedly turn away from the small nudges of loved ones, desperate souls at points in life never intended.

In shock and dismay, they face a bankruptcy attorney.

Confused, they face the actions of an angry, disrespectful, and defiant teenager.

Dazed and distraught, the day comes where the accumulation of items over a fifteen–year marriage are divided into two homes coupled with the fact that they will only see their children three days out of seven. "I told myself I would never get a divorce" are the words uttered.

Shocked and stunned, friends and family remark, "They were the perfect couple."

Many experience this as if it came out of the blue. It never comes out of the blue. It is always a slow and steady burn, the consistent turning of a stubborn shoulder away from one another that results in the corrosion of relationship. It is in the not paying attention to the cry of the wife to not work so much and come home. It is in the closing of the ears when a husband feels criticized and abandoned by his wife. Divorce is, in many cases, the aftermath of a long line of turning away from that place where we know we ought not to turn away. Free will is the issue. A consistent "no" must be respected.

Hardening the Heart

> But they refused to pay attention and turned a stubborn shoulder and stopped their ears from hearing. They made their hearts like flint so that they could not hear the law and the words which the Lord of hosts had sent by His Spirit through the former prophets.
> **Zechariah 7:11–12**

Consistent turning away is referred to in scripture as a "hardening the heart." Hardness of the heart is not a one–time event, but many turns away from the small movements of the Holy Spirit. These turns cause a searing to the sensitivity of God's presence. I am not suggesting that we can lose salvation. That would suggest that we can gain it. I am suggesting that we have free will, and it is that free will that is a variable in the level of our intimacy with God and others.

Yesterday, I got to see my heart on a sonogram. My doctor was being extra cautious because of a heart murmur. It was really cool to see my heart pumping. I went home and told my husband about it.

He commented, "Isn't it interesting that the heart doesn't get tired for around eighty years?"

I looked puzzled.

He reminded me, "The heart is just a muscle. All muscles get tired. The heart works nonstop for seventy to eighty years plus and doesn't get tired."

Indeed, our heart is a strong muscle—it takes a lot to harden it. It takes a lot of abuse, a lot of little moments of ignoring and a lot of damage before it will actually harden. This is certainly true of the hardening of our hearts toward God.

THE CRAVING FOR SIGNS

But He answered and said to them, "An evil and adulterous generation craves for a sign; and yet no sign will be given to it but the sign of Jonah the prophet."
Matthew 12:39

In the above verse, Jesus refers to our natural inclination to be drawn toward the flashy and dramatic. We are attracted to, and even desire, a grand showing of miracles.

Jesus was healing the sick, giving sight to blind, and raising the dead.

It wasn't enough. It wasn't enough because it would never be enough. In fact, in Matthew 12:39 He seems to be talking about hearts so hardened that even grand signs or miracles will not make an impact.

Standing before Jesus were the Pharisees and Sadducees. They were talking to the living, breathing word of God—the living manifestation of the scriptures they had memorized. The miracles Jesus performed were the very miracles that identified Him as the Messiah. Even a synagogue's official's daughter had been resurrected by Jesus (Mark 5). Only God could open the eyes of the blind, unstop the ears of the deaf, strengthen the legs of the lame, free the tongue of the mute, and raise the dead from darkness.

Then will the eyes of the blind be opened and the ears of
the deaf unstopped. Then will the lame leap like a deer, and
the mute tongue shout for joy. Water will gush forth in the
wilderness and streams in the desert.
Isaiah 35:5–6 (NIV)

The Spirit of the Sovereign LORD is on me, because the
LORD has anointed me to proclaim good news to the poor.
He has sent me to bind up the brokenhearted, to proclaim
freedom for the captives and release from darkness for the
prisoners.
Isaiah 61:1 (NIV)

Nicodemus, a member of the Pharisees, said they (the Pharisees)
knew where Jesus came from and who He was. Yet they were so hardened and seared in that place of knowing that they could not accept
the Messiah standing before them. When a person stands in the face
of God's call and denies the petition, there is a searing of conscience, a
hardening of the heart.

Stephen from the early church, filled with the Holy Spirit, spoke
to this hardening of hearts. Knowing that He was preaching the truth,
the Sanhedrin had to produce the testimony of a false witness to even
capture and hold Stephen. After the false testimony, Stephen was asked
if he had something to say.

In the face of his inevitable death, he told the Sanhedrin that they
are denying the truth of God—standing before them—as their fathers
have done from the beginning of time. He told of the history of ancient
Israel and the hardening of hearts. He spoke of the ageless rejection of
the truth that is set before them. The God they worshiped was right before them with undeniable truth and they hung Him on a cross.

After Stephen spoke the truth, they screamed and covered their
ears. Then they grabbed hold of him and stoned him.

No one can be in the presence of God, the living Word of God, or the written Word of God and not be changed. The heart will be changed; the question is whether it will be hardened or convicted. Hardened, it will be unreceptive to the very living presence of God—to the gentle whispering of the Holy Spirit, who speaks truth not of Himself but of God the Father. Convicted, the heart becomes transformed to the heart of the Father. A declination changes everything because it is one step further away from the Holy Trinity.

In Revelation 3:20, Jesus says that He stands at the door of our life and knocks; it is our choice to answer or ignore the knock. Matthew tells us of a time when the door will be opened and that there will be a time when the door is shut. "Yet later, the other virgins also came, saying, 'Lord, lord, open up for us.' But He answered, 'Truly I say to you, I do not know you'" (Matthew 25:11-12 NASB).

Filtering the Invitation through a Distorted Self

Questioned and pondered throughout the span of man, the self is an intricate world of great light and darkness, embedded with fear, hope, pain, faith, joy, and sorrow. It is capable of great delusion, great sacrifice, great love, great hate, and great clarity. It is within this mass of competing forces that for seventy–plus years, we make our choices for harm or good. As we meander through our timeline, the questions "Who am I?" and "Why do I do what I do?" have haunted and will continue to haunt the heart of man.

Though complicated, a right understanding of self is an important matter with significant implications:

- Self, understood from a kingdom perspective, changes how we approach evangelism, missions, service, family, marriage, child rearing, church relationships, and relationship with God.
- Self, rightly understood, reveals a life free of condemnation (Romans 8:1), promotes an approach to sin that re-

moves the ineffective use of "willpower," orients a life into the "easy yoke," leads a life into kingdom humility, guides a life lived out of our unique gifts and talents, frees a life from comparing self to others, and leads a life to extraordinary transformation.

- Self, rightly understood, frees us from works–based faith into faith–generated works. Set free from self-obsession, we are liberated to cooperate with the dynamic work of the Holy Spirit and not our work. Set free from the expectations or concerns of others, we are let loose to live a life radically centered in the unpredictable, unimaginable will of God. Set free from our human desired outcomes, we live in extraordinary kingdom outcomes.

Paradigms designed to comprehend the complexity of the "self" are numerous.

Some devout, well–meaning theology has suggested that any pursuit of empowering self is in direct conflict with scripture that speaks of denying the flesh (Matthew 16:24, 25; Mark 8:34, 35; Luke 9:23, 24). Jeremiah 17:9 certainly tells us that the heart is desperately wicked. The Apostle Paul reminds us that there is "no one righteous, no not one" (Romans 3:10).

Unfortunately, this two–dimensional approach to this important and complicated matter of self has been the fuel of burn-out, self-righteousness, anxiety, depression, and disillusionment. Paradoxically, this theological orientation of denying self can itself become a form of idolatry, much like the Pharisees who were so intent on tithing, which became the thing worshiped (Matthew 23:23). The other end of the spectrum is equally unhealthy and harmful, a view of self that is held with such primary focus that everything(one) comes second.

Neither come close to the kingdom power and freedom of a right view of self. Not only does scripture support a healthy perspective on self but Jesus also modeled it for us.

This is an adaptation of the classic model of true self/false self. The self will be identified in three parts: the false self, the distorted self, and the true self.

The True Self

Your true self is what was originally designed, the original blueprint, if you will. Knit in your mother's womb by the very hand of God (Psalm 139), made on purpose (Romans 8:29), known deeply (Psalm 94:11), delighted in (Psalm 37:23), this is the true self. It is here in cooperative activity with the Holy Spirit the true self is being sanctified and transformed into the image of Christ. The creator, if we allow Him, is forming us into the fullness of who we were designed to be. He alone knows what that is. It is this true self that is hid in Christ, hid in God. It is this life that emerges as we set our mind on the things that are above, not on things of the earth (Colossians 3:3). It is this life that we are invited to cooperatively cultivate as we intimately interact and engage with the God that intentionally designed our unique being for this unique moment in time.

> For me to be a saint means to be myself. Therefore the problem of sanctity and salvation is in fact the problem of finding out who I am and of discovering my true self. Trees and animals have no problem. God makes them what they are without consulting them, and they are perfectly satisfied.

> With us it is different. God leaves us free to be whatever we like. We can be ourselves or not, as we please. Our vocation is not simply to be, but to work together with God in the creation of our own life, our own identity, our own destiny. To work out our own identity in God, which the Bible calls "working out our salvation," is a labor that requires sacrifice and anguish, risk and many tears. It demands close attention to reality at

every moment and great fidelity to God as He reveals Himself, obscurely, in the mystery of each new situation. We do not know clearly beforehand what the result of this work will be. The secret of my full identity is hidden in Him. "He alone can make me who I am, or rather who I will be when at last I fully begin to be." (Merton, *Seeds of Contemplation*, pp. 33, 34-35)

The Distorted Self

The distorted self is an inaccurate, damaged conceptualization of self. Formed through lies, judgments, misunderstandings, incorrect conclusions, condemnations, trauma, and manipulations, the distorted self is a compilation of half-truths and untruths that are held as true. Most folks live a majority of their lives from this distorted place, the place of our greatest fears. We fear we are not good enough. We fear we are unlovable. We fear we aren't smart enough. We believe we aren't attractive enough. There are some generic fears we all carry, but then there are some specific fears that we carry, usually related to specific trauma. Maybe you're too tall to be attractive to any man. Maybe you're too poor to ever be successful. Maybe your only value is how you look. There are as many variations as there are human stories. The distorted self is a painful place to pay attention to—so we don't. To compensate for this pain, we create masks, defense mechanisms. . . the false self.

The False Self

Masks or defense mechanisms hide what we fear is true about us from the world. So to compensate for feeling "not smart enough," we use big words or get degree after degree. We may believe we are inherently not good enough, so we focus our life's energies in having the perfect house, car, family to compensate for this dark pain. We feel profoundly unlovable, so we learn to use sexual relationships to have moments of acceptance. We are afraid we are the failure our father told us we would become so we spend a lifetime achieving in order to compensate for that pain. The false self serves at the pleasure of the distorted self. It protects and serves the distorted self in an attempt to resolve all the unpleasant and unwanted characteristics.

The Samaritan Woman at the Well

Most of us read the scripture the way we read cellphone texts—through the filter of condemnation, harshness, judgment, and anger. This is not about Jesus; this is about our filter. The woman at the well (John 4) is an iconic example as she interacts with Jesus. Jesus approaches her with objectivity, reflection, curiosity, compassion, and truth. She, however, responds with defensiveness, judgement, and anger.

> There came a woman of Samaria to draw water. Jesus said to her, "Give Me a drink." For His disciples had gone away into the city to buy food. Therefore the Samaritan woman said to Him, "How is it that You, being a Jew, ask me for a drink since I am a Samaritan woman? (For Jews have no dealings with Samaritans.)
> **John 4:7–9**

Societal exposure had told this woman that she was less than all Jews and all males. We do not know all the details of her story, but we find later that she had five husbands. A woman who has had five husbands has drawn some false conclusions about her constitutive value.

Jesus challenges this wrongly translated exposure. He audaciously speaks to her as if she were equally valuable. By the very act of talking to this woman, Jesus begins to break down her wrongly formed conclusions of her value as a Samaritan and as a woman.

By starting to break down her distorted self, He begins opening the door to transformation of her true self. He pierces all the way down to who she really is, and she sees it.

And she says yes.

Jesus' Response to Our Distorted and False Selves

GENTLE AS WE GO

Plumbing the depths of who we are is a challenging task. It is here that we must take our time and approach with objectivity, compassion, and kindness. Formed through a lifetime of lies, misinformation, attack, pain, trauma, and hurt, the false self has become highly adapted, honed, and reinforced as our first line of defense.

The false self engages with life on guard and on alert for attack. Consider our approach to other drivers on the road; all actions are viewed as threats to our general safety. This operates much like the well–honed false self protecting the distorted self. How many fights have occurred because a text is read with a negative and defensive filter?

When we consider what others might think of us, it is rare for us to come to positive conclusions. We are defensive and hurting fearful people engaging with other defensive and hurting fearful people attempting relationship, the thing we all deeply crave but are fearful of.

Our wounded and hurting distorted self has learned over time that it is not safe to come out and play because of the constant onslaught of attack. One must approach gently, because any aggressive approach alerts all defensive mechanisms and will often hijack any attempt.

Jesus knew this. Jesus engaged with the world gently. When we begin to read Jesus' words with a gentle and compassionate voice, the entire meaning changes. "Oh, ye of little faith"—once read as a booming voice of condemnation, we can now hear as a compassionate concern: "Hey, guys, why the doubt? Where's your faith?" Didn't Jesus call these gentlemen His friends? I don't yell condemnation at my friends that I love. I might challenge a friend struggling with an issue that she is going through with an obvious question, "Oh, really, what's that about?" She knows that I know her, and it is out of that knowing that I can ask the poignant question.

Objectivity, reflection, curiosity, compassion, and truth are the tools we need. These are the tools that Jesus used when He walked this earth and engaged with our hurting parts. This is the most effective way to not only navigate the false self and distorted self but also to enable access and understanding of the true self.

It also helps to have an understanding of how our false and distorted selves came about. How did this even happen?

THE FORMING OF THE SELF

Humans are voracious data–consuming machines. Accurate or inaccurate, data is received as early as in the womb. The least impacted by data, and typically not yet defended against the world, children draw us into their honesty because they work out of what is truest about themselves. They do not operate out of any concept of good or bad; they just are who they are. Their selfish natures, generous hearts, playful souls, demanding attitudes, insatiable capacity for love and unquenchable need to dance, children are the purest form of this human condition. It doesn't last long, as they are sponges that begin to assimilate data from exposure; a "self" is being formed.

Our self is formed through a combination of input, interpretation, and integration.

Input is the information we are assailed with from the earliest moments of life. Input continues endlessly. From conception we receive input both physically and emotionally. In the womb we are impacted by data from the mother from what she inhales, eats, experiences, feels, etc. We are then propelled into a world of data: nurses, doctors, needles, blankets, lights, skin to skin, sight, loud noises, some familiar voices, milk. . . so much data and there is so much more to come. Media, culture, friends, siblings, iPods, iPads, siblings, more noise, more people, more messages about who we are and who we are not. Does your world tell you that you're fat, short, talented, gifted, too loud, in need of punishment, too tall, not funny, ugly, good, or bad? Inundated with data, the self is being formed.

Messages and data from our culture, family, church, community, and friends can be accurate or skewed. Accurate messages contribute to the forming of our true selves. Distorted messages contribute to the forming of our distorted self.

We are not completely at the mercy of incoming data—how we choose to interpret that incoming data also plays a big role. In fact, it is not the data that primarily shapes us but our interpretation and integration of the data.

Some data has a default, almost automatic interpretation. For example, violence is automatically categorized as painful and bad, while pleasurable data is defined as good. Other data is dismissed (Crazy Aunt Lulu is. . . well, she is crazy).

The rest of the information is interpreted. And for folks without healthy assistance, interpretation and organization of data can get significantly distorted.

Data interpreted and integrated without judgment becomes a part of the true self. The true self is shaped in a safe, non-anxious, nonjudgmental, accurate environment.

The distorted self, however, is shaped from data—both inaccurate and accurate—that is experienced in an unsafe environment marked by shame, guilt, judgment, and violence, whether that violence is emotional, spiritual, physical, or psychological.

How we integrate—or act on—our interpretations is a third piece of the puzzle.

Raised in an environment where questions are met with frustration, ridicule, or irritation, a child may develop a distorted self that believes curiosity and questions are bad. The false self will now act on that lie and suppress the true self's curiosity. But this protective strategy hijacks a critical developmental skill. Curiosity and exploration are critical to mastering our environment, which leads to many important developmental phases including autonomy, initiative, industry, and so many more. This has significant implications in all areas of life including how to prepare for adulthood, whom to pick as a mate, and eventually parenting.

Children, by virtue of their developmental level, are less capable of interpreting and integrating data in healthy ways. How many children with learning disabilities begin to believe they are unintelligent because of their placement in "special" classes? How many dyslexic children never live up to their full potential because they buy into the lie that they aren't as smart as their peers? This is when parents, adults, counselors, and teachers step in and help children process the exposure.

But children are not alone.

The disempowered among us suffer because often there is no way to help process the exposure properly. Immigrants, the disabled, the elderly, the disenfranchised are all susceptible to exposure that inaccurately processed can become the distorted self. Deprivation of information, severe trauma, extended periods of time with disinformation, abuse, poverty, and other factors prevent the incorporation of exposure in healthy ways. The inability to process exposure in healthy ways creates dysfunctional outcomes: lies, misunderstandings, false beliefs, insecurity, paralyzing

fear, distortions, defense mechanisms, addictions, anger, self-harm, suicide, murder, hate, violence, abuse. . . all these are foundation blocks of
the distorted self.

THE FALSE SELF: THE ILLUSION

To Serve

The false self is driven to identify and meet the needs of the distorted self. Considering that the distorted self is generally formed out of
pain, fear, lies and trauma, the false self will be equally distorted in its
service.

For example, the false self might seek an unwanted career in order
to earn the bigger income to shore up belief that we must achieve the
status of our brother, father, or neighbor in order to be acceptable.

In order to resolve the distorted belief that we are unlovable, the
false self may justify the choice to dive into an untested relationship
knowing at a deeper level that this is a repeating of old unhealthy patterns.

In order to compensate for the belief of inevitable rejection, the
false self will choose another drink to strengthen courage.

The drive to meet the needs of our wounded distorted self is a
powerful energy that drives us to bizarre and exaggerated behaviors. We
know they are unhealthy and damaging, but the drive is stronger. Even
in the face of wise advice and feedback from trusted loved ones, the false
self can make dangerous choices in service of distorted self.

Let's go back for a moment to the story of the Samaritan woman.
We can immediately see how her response to Jesus' question was to defend and protect herself. Serving the deeper distorted truth that she was
not worthy and that people are dangerous, the Samaritan woman was at
first protective then aggressive and defensive in the face of the thing she
really wanted. Jesus is offering her real and lasting relationship, which
she had attempted to attain through marriage. We do not know how she

got to this position in life. It could have been her choices or the exposure of society, but more likely both. We just know she is broken and hurting.

As Jesus was wont to do, He intentionally sought out the broken, the lost, and the outcast. As always when engaging with these folks, whether the woman caught in adultery, Zacchaeus, lepers, Peter's sick mother, or this lost and hurting Samaritan woman, Jesus came with objectivity, reflection, curiosity, compassion, and truth. It is only this service of love that can combat the service of the false self, heal the broken heart of the distorted self, and enter the true self created by God.

Destroys Relationship

Seeking resolution to pain, the false self is in service only to the distorted self and is disinterested in the needs of another unless it feeds the self-interest of the distorted self. The work of the false self can be so intensely driven by the distorted self's shame, guilt, and insecurity that awareness of the impact on others goes unnoticed. Remember, lies are a common contributor to the shaping of a distorted self. The father of lies is at work in the distorted self.

A common distortion that destroys relationships and is held tightly by many Christians is the distortion around anger (Ephesians 4:26). In many cases, being angry has been adopted as part of the distorted self as bad. "If I am angry, then I am a bad sinner."

Anger is a hard thing and because it most often has unpleasant consequences, we wrap it in shame and guilt, label it sin, and store it in the distorted self. Because of this the "good Christian" can't get angry and the false self has to work diligently to prevent any possible anger due to the misconception that God will be displeased.

For a Christian who passionately desires to please the Lord, this is untenable. Anger, a common, dangerous, and healthy part of being human, has now become a sin. The Christian who becomes angry may feel shame and guilt because the distorted self draws the conclusion that they are bad. The false self kicks in to protect from this pain and so slapping a

smile on our face, we call it "joy in the Lord" and begin to speak of forgiveness. Soon the sun is about to set so we better resolve this argument.

This illustration of anger demonstrates how the false self limits and
can actually destroy relationship. What we end up with are a bunch of
smiling, but furious, Christians who can't move because we can't resolve
any disagreements. This results in the destruction of community, which
limits relationship with God because God is a God of community (Matthew 5:24). All masks driven by the distorted self destroy relationships
because the relationship is interacting with something fake. Reminiscent
of Jesus' words that we should build a house not on sand but on a rock,
building relationships on the false self will not stand the test of time. But
relationships built on the true self have a foundation that can weather
the inevitable storms of life. Fake is fake.

The true self understands that anger is not only normal but necessary. Anger is just what it is. It is anger; there is no value judgment.
Anger is an invaluable flag that identifies areas that we get jammed up
in. Anger seeks justice. Anger can seek righteousness.

> "There is among the passions an anger of the intellect, and
> this anger is in accordance with nature. Without anger a man
> cannot attain purity: he has to feel angry with all that is sown
> in him by the enemy."
> **St. Nikodimos of the Holy Mountain, 1979**

If anger is used and understood appropriately, it actually can lead
to closer, deeper relationships with God, our true self, and one another.

Distorted self: The Darkness

Individuals who suffer from a poor image of themselves are
caught up in self-rejection and have no defenses against group
pressures. They do not see themselves as the objects of God's
love, and they have no place to make a stand. Henri Nouwen

noted, "Success, popularity and power can indeed present a great temptation, but their seductive quality often comes from the way they are part of a much larger temptation of self-rejection. When we have come to believe in the voices that call us worthless and unlovable, then success, popularity and power are easily perceived as attractive solutions" to our desolate condition. We accept it as a fact that we deserve to be pushed aside and rejected. We see ourselves that way.

"Self-rejection," Nouwen continued, "is the greatest enemy of the spiritual life because it contradicts the sacred voice that calls us the 'Beloved.' Being the Beloved constitutes the core truth of our existence." But this profound truth will have little or no effect without powerful images of ourselves as God's beloved. Self-rejection is, ultimately, our soul's reproach to God, deriving from false images of Himself and His world. (Willard, *Renovation of the Heart*, p. 101)

Lies, half-truths, truths, mistruths, misunderstandings, fear—all filtered with guilt, judgment, condemnation, and shame are building blocks to our distorted self. Much like those circus mirrors that contort our reflection into funny shapes, the distorted self might be a reflection but it is most certainly a skewed and wrong one. We know not to trust circus mirrors as accurate reflections; we may have more difficulty with life's distorted mirror.

Focused on Self and Centered in Other

Protect, serve, and defend, the false self is the diligent and faithful servant of the distorted self. Hyper-focused, the distorted self is clamoring for what it desperately needs. Being other-person centered means that other people define who you are and only they can resolve your pain.

The truly exhausting fact is that the distorted self only understands self based upon what the person in front of them reflects is true or isn't true. We see this often in high school–aged children. This is when developmentally they can be strongly susceptible to culture and peers. These sources tell them how they are supposed to look, what they are supposed to believe, how they are supposed to behave. This is true throughout our culture but is heightened in these tender years. We have all seen the distorted images of men and women who go through extraordinary and painful procedures to be acceptable to the culture they live in. This is not a judgment but a painful reflection. If we are honest, each and every one of us fall prey to this activity to one degree or another. This leaves the self exhausted, fearful, hyper-anxious, and ever hopeful that someone out there will somehow give them what they need. Like every other drug, conforming to others or getting confirmation from others meets a need in the moment but only leaves us with the aftermath of needing more and more.

Receiving information from other people about who we are is critical for our transformation and community relationships. It is when this is the primary and singular source of information that leads to a distorted self.

Truly Tricky

This drive of the distorted self can be camouflaged as good works, humility, sacrifice, confidence, or success. Breaking from the false self then becomes even more challenging because the feedback from the world is so rewarding. The motives of the false self are not only camouflaged to the world; they are often hidden from the person. It can be a hard thing to discern the deeper hidden motives of our actions. Adding to this difficulty is the fact that the drives of the distorted self can be hidden with good and pure motives. Sadly, as Paul says, "a little leaven works through the whole batch." Are our actions motivated by recognition, praise of others, glory of heaven, or to feel better about self? This is a hard question.

Red Flags

Frustration, resentment, anger, and discontent can be flags that the distorted self is not getting its needs met. Another sign can be when we feel a compelling need to set someone straight. When there is a need to recite a resume in the middle of a conversation, the distorted self is alive and active. Jesus identified the drive of the false self for recognition in the Pharisees when He said, "But they do all their deeds to be noticed by men; for they broaden their phylacteries and lengthen the tassels of their garments. They love the place of honor at banquets and the chief seats in the synagogues, and respectful greetings in the market places, and being called Rabbi by men" (Matthew 23:5–7).

Notice how their intention was to be noticed by men. This is a clear indicator that they are working out of false self driven by distorted self. It only takes a quick look at the Red Carpet, Congress, or the Real Housewives to realize nothing much has changed since then. We can see how those in the public eye are living out of the distorted self.

Wrongly Integrated

Acquisition and integration of data is what forms all parts of ourselves, as discussed earlier. Exposure interpreted and integrated wrongly creates the distorted self. When I was in first grade, I didn't make the best of grades. The teacher told my mother that some students are just average students, referring to me. My mother proceeded to tell her friends what the teacher said within ear shot. I spent the next fifteen years believing that I could not achieve much more than a C average.

I was a senior in college (barely by the looks of my GPA) and a friend remarked how smart I was. I looked at him, almost irritated that he spoke those words. "What?" was my response. With shock in his voice and a smile on his face he stated, "Oh, you don't know you are smart." My understanding of myself that day started to shift. A part of my distorted self had been challenged and found faulty. It was a slow process but my grades from that day forward shifted dramatically. I approached reading differently. I approached class differently. I approached homework differently.

I am not an average student. I am an *A* student. In fact, I came to find out that I am pretty smart. My first–grade teacher was trying to be helpful, as was my mom, but they were both completely wrong. Data was received and integrated incorrectly. My distorted self believed for years that I wasn't smart and so I continued to filter data through this truth. So if someone playfully said, "Were you born under a rock?" I would believe they were referring to my inferior intellect as opposed to a funny comment that suggested there was some common information that I did not know. My response now, in order to join in the humor, is "Yes, under a rock and in a barn." I take the comment for what it is. . . a joke! That distortion is cleared up.

Tricky Truth

Perceived as reality, the distorted self is sadly where most people live and have their being ever only to hear faint wishful echoes of the true self.

Reverberating in our dreamy ideas, wishful hopes, and big ideas, we often can get a glimpse of the magnitude of the true self. When we can for a moment mute the false and distorted self to hear the true self, we soar with hope and clarity.

Then we come back to what we call "reality" and live our lives driven by self-doubt, self-condemnation, and false confidence. The distorted self is imprisoned in a cell of circus mirrors constantly reminding us of our failings and limitations.

I do not know if it is true, but there is an old story that serves as a great metaphor. The story explains that the way that circus elephants are trained and controlled is that when they are young, they are bound by the leg with irons that are tied to the center circus tent pole. At this young age, the tent pole prevents them from running away. As they mature and become strong, powerful animals that could easily pull down a circus tent, they now only have a rope tied to their ankle. The animal has been trained to believe and experience has proven that they are not strong enough to pull down a tent pole. They never consider it. A striking story of living in darkness.

Rooted in the anxiety of the false self to protect the insecure distorted self, we center on what other folks say is acceptable to God, not what God declares Himself. Our theology homilized as freedom, liberty, and life–altering power yet corrals adherents through the fear of hell, the guilt of sin, and the shame of the "not getting it right" promotes a life bifurcated in Christ, a life disempowered of the horsepower of Heaven. This theology of fear fuels the false and distorted self to become protective and hide, thereby jumpstarting the work of the false self to create a presentation that will be found acceptable.

And Christian hypocrisy is born. Working nonstop, the false self better get it right—wear the right length skirt, say the right prayer, have the right haircut, worship the right way, and gosh darn it (Oops, is that a euphemism?), don't ever get angry. So, in order to be a good Christian and escape the fiery flames of hell, the distorted self learns how to fit in and become acceptable.

This isn't transformation; this is adaptation and conformity. This is human–driven and not Holy Spirit–driven change. The distorted self knows that if anyone really knew who was under the presentation, they would kick him out of the club for sure. The false self begins its service; a mask is born and a new club member is on the rolls.

I think it helpful to be reminded from time to time that Jesus was not acceptable to church administration. Christian lives lived out of false selves are not driven out of a power of the living God but the power of the distorted self's anxiety to get past the bar. Fear begets fear begets fear begets fear. We were not designed to hold fear at our core, as Timothy reminds us when he wrote, "For God gave us not a spirit of fearfulness; but of power and love and discipline" (2 Timothy 1:7 ASV).

Christianity doesn't appear to be a life of freedom but more like a life of hard labor and servitude. Who would want this kind of life and have it in abundance?

So here's where the rubber meets the road. Here's the question that gets to the heart of everything: What if Christianity was an invitation into the true self, into the self that was knit in your mother's womb by the hand of heaven (Psalm 139), into a life made in the image of God?

What if Christianity is an invitation to live life with Jesus as He lived as His disciple without condemnation, in unlimited grace, endless compassion, and truth?

What would it look like if we lived our life out of the spirit of power, love, and discipline?

CHAPTER 6

God Invites Us into Our True Selves

The inner self is not an ideal self, especially not an imaginary, perfect creature fabricated to measure up to our compulsive need for greatness, heroism, and infallibility. On the contrary, the real "I" is simply our self. Nothing more, nothing less. Our self as we are in the eyes of God, to use Christian terms. Our self in all our uniqueness, dignity, littleness, and ineffable greatness: the greatness we have received from God our Father and what we share with Him because He is our Father and "in Him we live and move and have our being" (Acts 17:28 NIV) (Merton, *The Inner Experience,* p. 11).

Truth really does set us free.

Living from the true self is not living a life free of problems, all dreams fulfilled and challenges gone, but living a life unencumbered from self-criticism and self-condemnation, free to face life's challenges in the power of what is true.

With no judgment, no standard to meet, no guilt, no shame, no condemnation, no power struggle, we are free to ponder, grow, and change. We can be curious about possibilities; seek compassion, kindness, and clarity; seek and know truth; and build relationships with God, self, and one another.

One of the most life–giving attributes of living from our true self is that we let go of manipulating others' lives to get them to be, believe, or do what we think is right for them because we don't need them to validate ourselves. The implications are staggering. Freed from manipulating others' spiritual lives, we are free to journey with one another as we each journey with God, trusting that He is guiding each person. Free to share confession and reflection, and even correction, without manipulation.

What would it look like to have a group of people who were not invested in who is in control of which committee, not invested in who agrees with who about what doctrine, but invested in the journey of each other's lives as they individually in community follow the path that God has set before them?

> It's who you are and the way you live that count before God. Your worship must engage your spirit in the pursuit of truth. That's the kind of people the Father is out looking for: those who are simply and honestly themselves before him in their worship. God is sheer being itself—Spirit. Those who worship him must do it out of their very being, their spirits, their true selves, in adoration.
> **John 4:23–24** (MSG)

To rightly understand our true self, we must return to the original relationship we had with God—*before the whisper.*

BEFORE THE WHISPER

Before the serpent's whisper, Adam and Eve lived with God. Scripture never says that Adam and Eve were perfect—good but not perfect. The idea was that in relationship, He would develop them—much like the development of our children.

Before the serpent's whisper, Adam and Eve had access and power over everything that they could possibly see except for one tree. Inherent in the exception of the tree was an invitation to cooperatively work together with God as they managed the kingdom of the garden. Inherent in the exception of the tree was an invitation to conversation. Possibly inherent in the exception of the tree, God was inviting conversation that promotes intimacy. When I withhold things from my children, I encourage them to ask. The ask allows for conversation and teachable moments. We talk until they understand the limitation. Generally speaking those limitations are just for now and not forever. In the conversation, the children come to understand the love, protection, and care we have for them. This promotes closeness. I wonder what would have happened if instead of eating of the tree, Eve decided to have a conversation and say, "Hey, I was told this other thing. What do you think?"

We are invited back to that place before the whisper. The before the whisper place is where we get the privilege of working cooperatively with the Holy Spirit, fulfilling the will of God for the life initiated at our conception which always was intended to be grown and matured into the image and maturity of Jesus Christ. It is here that we know who we are truly because we know who God is.

Who God Is Defines Who We Are

God is love. Let me be clear on the definition of love I am using. "Love is not a feeling, or a special way of feeling, but the divine way of relating to others and oneself that moves through every dimension of our being and restructures our world for good" (Willard, 2011). By definition, God is for good. Accepting that God is for good is a grand thing with significant implications. Who He is defines who we are.

We say the words and sing the songs, but our lives reveal the truth of what we believe. We are told we are children of the Most High God, but we live as if we are unwanted, unliked, disinherited stepchildren.

This is all so simple to say, and we all nod our heads in agreement, but here is the ugly truth: understanding who we really are doesn't happen by getting dipped or sprinkled and repeating some words.

Understanding who we are (children of the Most High God) takes disciplined training of repeatedly/continually placing ourselves before the throne of God where we let God do the work of healing our distorted and false self and complete the work He started in the true self before the whisper. It is the disciplined work of facing the totality of God's love, as best we can, and coming to terms with not only who He is, but who we are in that context.

In a world where hyperbolic language is the norm, we have lost the meaning of words like love and good. I love my children. It is certainly a feeling, an overwhelming feeling that makes me cry. (I am a sappy mom.) However, it is more importantly my desire for their good that out of love I do the things that I do not want to do.

It is out of love that I correct my son on a white lie. The white lie had no impact on me in any way, but I know that a habit of lying can have a devastating impact in life from jobs to marriages. I work with adults all the time who through habitual lying have caused significant heartache in their lives. So I do the unpleasant task of confronting him and holding him accountable. Yuck! I really just wanted to get back to what I was doing and ignore the lie. It was, after all, a small one. But I couldn't ignore it because I have a strong desire for his good. I think similarly God corrects me, not because He is angry with my sin or He can't be in the presence of my sin, but because my sin hurts me and everyone around me, so He kindly comes alongside and whispers conviction. Ouch! Yikers! I didn't see that. But now that I do, I can act for good.

Living out of the true self is knowing that God is God, you are what He made, and it wasn't a mistake. It is here that we find we are defined by the love of God. Psalm 139 tells us that every part of the/

our self is known. Our entire self holds all of our fear, hope, pain, joy, and sorrow. This is where the Lord speaks into and defines who we are despite what we fear is true (distorted self). It is here that Jesus spoke to the woman found in adultery and said, "I don't condemn you." In her darkness, He shines His light of compassion.

It is in this light of compassion that we find His definition of who we truly are. It is not hard for us to identify as sinners. After all, there is a lot of evidence for the prosecution. Reminded that Satan is the accuser of the brethren, why do we go around working on his behalf to condemn ourselves? Why do we do his work for him? I am not suggesting that we don't confess our sins. I am suggesting that we don't orient who we are from there.

Our true selves have many other names besides sinner: Holy Priest, eternal precious child of the Most High God, the apple of the Creator's eye, judger of Angels, the redeemed of The Lord, a people made completely free forever, co-rulers in the Kingdom of God, inheritors of eternal life, the begotten of God. If these descriptors are true, then what does that change? If we are indeed set free, what are we free to do?

His Power: Good

Invited into a life in His power, we can begin to hear the sweet calling of a God who wants to be with us through all of our days. We begin to hear a God who delights in the details of our lives. We begin to hear a God who calls us to a path of freedom and goodness and cups overflowing. We hear a God whose heart is a heart that wants to bless. We hear a God who corrects because His heart is for our good. We begin to hear a God who says, "Please organize your life in such a way that you may live life well and that we might live it together." We hear a God who says, "Don't do these things, because in the end they will hurt you. They might feel good in the moment, but in the end they are poison." We hear a God who says, "Oh, pick these things to do. They are hard at first but in the end, it will be awesome." We hear a God who says, "Trust me. I got you."

We hear a God who says, "I will finish the work I started before the whisper, if you will but trust me."

For I am confident of this very thing, that He who began a good work in you will perfect it until the day of Christ Jesus.
Philippians 1:6

Who will also confirm you to the end, blameless in the day of our Lord Jesus Christ.
1 Corinthians 1:8

For we are His workmanship, created in Christ Jesus for good works, which God prepared beforehand so that we would walk in them.
Ephesians 2:10

You also, as living stones, are being built up as a spiritual house for a holy priesthood, to offer up spiritual sacrifices acceptable to God through Jesus Christ.
1 Peter 2:5

Listen to Me, O house of Jacob,
And all the remnant of the house of Israel,
You who have been borne by Me from birth
And have been carried from the womb;
Even to your old age I will be the same,
And even to your graying years I will bear you!
I have done it, and I will carry you;
And I will bear you and I will deliver you.
Isaiah 46:3–4

"I will always be with you; will you be with me?" (Foster, 2009-10-13) He desires to be with you in relationship so that He can love you. He desires to be in relationship with you so that He can do good for you. He desires to be in relationship with you so that we can go back to where we were designed to be—before the whisper.

SHARED LIFE: INTIMACY

As it was in the garden so is it now; God desires intimate relationship. Before the whisper, Adam and Eve were being invited to engage in intimate relationship with their Creator as they enjoyed the garden together. They were so familiar with this community that scripture says God was walking in the cool of the day (Genesis 3:8). They were in communal relationship.

Just as we agree to marry another, we engage in the wedding ceremony, a covenant, a one–time event, but then we engage in a lifetime process of intricate communion. A relationship where we know the slightest curve in one another's bodies, a negligible change in tone of voice, a mild change in concern is the nature of intimacy. It is where we know, and we know that we know. This is *yada*.

This can only be learned through time spent together and communication with all its variations. Intimacy is the practiced and matured knowledge and experience of another's soul seeking mutual pleasure, whether that is physical, mental, emotional, or spiritual.

Relationship is the point; it has always been the point.

In choosing relationship with God, we choose to interact with Him and adjust our lives to Him as we figure this thing out together. Otherwise, it is not a relationship but an agreed–upon arrangement.

When we marry another person, most aspects of our lives change. We must adjust to sleeping patterns, eating patterns, friends, housework, finances—almost all aspects of our lives adjust to the living, dynamic movement of our mate because we are figuring this thing out together. Then, oh my, the adjustments when a little person joins the house. That is intimate relationship.

This is true of our relationship with the Lord. He isn't an immovable object that has all the marbles, and you have to play His game, His way. This is not a contract two parties agree to. In fact, quite the contrary, He has invited us to do this thing together, to spend time together, and to learn of each other—to *yada*. He already loves us; His invitation is for us to know Him.

In loving Him, we grow in intimate relationship with Him. In growing into intimate relationship with Him, we want to obey (John 14:15) and please Him because we know that He loves us, and by definition that means He only wants what is good for us. This can only be known if we spend time with Him. It is in this process of spending time with Him that we learn of Him, that we hear His voice.

> God knows best what we need. All that He does is for our good. If we knew how much He loves us, we would always be ready to receive both the bitter and the sweet from His hand. It would make no difference. All that came from Him would be pleasing. The worst afflictions only appear intolerable if we see them in the wrong light. When we see them as coming from the hand of God and know that it is our loving Father who humbles and distresses us, our sufferings lose their bitterness and can even become a source of consolation. (Lawrence, *The Collected Works,* 2008)

Time together cultivates sensitivity and suppleness to the slightest breath of the other.

The other day I was sitting in a chair with my back to the base of the stairs. One of my kids was coming down the stairs. I couldn't figure who it was until I heard them breathe. I knew who it was because I have listened to the cadence of that breath for well over a decade. I knew because that child has been held close.

Sensitivity to the breath and movement of God is intimacy. Will we hear Him, or will we not notice His breathing? Elijah ran away to a cave, and God did not come in the fire or the storm but in a whisper. It is in a whisper that God reached down to His beloved prophet. It is in His whispers that He reaches down to us, His beloved.

Jesus' invitation isn't characterized by domination, power, condemnation, and shame. That's what we do. He uses words like easy yoke and friendship. He invites the tired and weary to receive rest. He fed people and healed terminal diseases; He sought out the poor, abandoned, and rejected of the world. He seems like a gent most of us would admire and want to know. His table is an offering of mercy, grace, forgiveness, and love for all who come. He invites us to follow Him. This is the God who beckons.

Enduringly persistent throughout the span of mankind, the invitation must be answered. The invitation has been extended.

"I am with you. Will you be with me?"

"I stand at the door and knock."

"Come, follow me."

"Abide in me."

"Choose life."

LOVE: AN INVITATION TO MAKE DINNER

Several years ago when my little Sarah was around seven, she asked if she could make dinner for the family. In gleeful anticipation of fun and enjoyment of this delight of a human being, I smiled and said, "Of course, what would you like to make for dinner?"

She rattled off a menu. Apparently she had given it some thought. So we proceeded to cook dinner for the family. Sarah, being so small, mostly salted this and that, correcting me along the way by saying, "That is not how Grandma salts things." We had a wonderful time stirring and talking and singing and salting. We brought it to the table and declared that this is the dinner that Sarah has made.

Let me ask you, who really made dinner? Well, for that moment in time, Sarah made the dinner. Sarah, in that moment, reveled in the reality that for the first time in her precious life, she had made dinner. I would not disagree. It was wonderful. It was a wonderful time and a more wonderful memory. It was by my power interactive with her power that dinner was made. She showed up and asked. I was thrilled.

God wants to make dinner with us. The invitation is there. Genesis to Revelation is an invitation, a letter, to His beloved, yet we open this wonderful letter from God and hear rules and demands. Is there any chance it is just an invitation to make dinner? It is not our works that He is deeply invested in. He doesn't need them. Remember, He can raise up stones (Matthew 3:9). He is invested in our presence with Him so that we can do this thing together. He knows the menu and is telling us how things work in the life for the best. He knows how to cook the potatoes so that we can have those beloved mashed potatoes. There are things that bring life and there are things that bring death. Choose life (Deuteronomy 30:19), please!

I am not trying to make light of the holiness of God nor sin, repentance, and redemption. These are matters of great importance, and there are folks much smarter (like my husband, the theologian) who can speak of these things. I am willingly open to learn and continue to grow. I am speaking to the mostly unspoken and very real distortion that we are called to "do for God." This is a grave distortion of power.

I am saying that we are called to be with God. It is not our works but His works that are produced from our interactive presence with Him, where He does the work of molding the pot and refining the metal. We just show up and interact with what He is doing. It is our desire to make dinner. It is in gleeful anticipation of fun and enjoyment of this delight of a human being that He smiles and says, "Of course, what would you like to make for dinner?"

CHAPTER 7

His Presence Changes Everything

But we all, with unveiled face, beholding as in a mirror the glo-
ry of the Lord, are being transformed into the same image from
glory to glory, just as from the Lord, the Spirit.
2 Corinthians 3:18

C hristian spiritual formation is the sustained habitual activity of beholding God with an unveiled face as He transforms us into the image of Jesus Christ. It is our choice to be present. It is our choice to orient our lives in such a way that we choose His divine gaze. It is our choice to listen and turn toward Him. It is all about our choice to cooperate with the movement of the divine Holy Spirit that magnetically lures us to the presence of God so that He might do the work that He started in us so very long ago.

A fearful, glorious, and intoxicating experience, the presence of the living eternal God sweetly invades the depth of our soul—the place beyond words, where we are shaken, undone, forever changed, and healed. It is in this presence, beyond words and most often in silence, the language of heaven, that one cannot but be changed—not changed in any way we could conjure up, but changed perfectly, rightly, and with sweet precision.

In the year that King Uzziah died, I saw the Lord sitting on a throne, high and lifted up, and the train of His robe filled the temple. Above it stood seraphim; each one had six wings; with two he covered his face, with two he covered his feet, and with two he flew. And one cried to another and said: "Holy, holy, holy is the LORD of hosts; The whole earth is full of His glory!" And the posts of the door were shaken by the voice of him who cried out, and the house was filled with smoke. Then I said: Woe is me, for I am undone! Because I am a man of unclean lips, And I dwell in the midst of a people of unclean lips; For my eyes have seen the King, The LORD of hosts.
Isaiah 6:1–5

Interestingly, I think that when Isaiah is in the presence of God, there is no interaction between God and Isaiah—just silence. The praise of the seraphim shook the door posts. The train of His robe and smoke filled the temple. It must have been an intoxicating, overwhelming experience for Isaiah to be at the throne of God. In the presence of the One True God, Isaiah was undone. *Strong's Concordance* defines the word as "to cease, cause to cease, cut off, destroy, perish." Isaiah had a sense of being destroyed by the presence of God. The pellucid, crushing, sweet, silent presence of the Lord of Hosts in one moment not only broke Isaiah but transformed him to see what he needed to see and then convicted Isaiah to go to Israel. God did not reveal every sin; He transformed Isaiah to see what he needed to see in order to go. It is this presence that we are invited into for the purposes of transformation.

It is an overwhelming experience to fall into the hands of the living God, to be invaded to the depths of our being by His presence, to be, without warning, wholly uprooted from all earthborn securities and assurances, and to be blown by a tempest of unbelievable power which leaves one's old proud self utterly, utterly defenseless, until one cries, "All Thy waves and thy billows are gone over me" (Psalm 42:7 KJV). Then is the soul swept into a Loving Center of ineffable sweetness, where calm and unspeakable peace and ravishing joy steal over one. (Kelly, *A Testament of Devotion,* 1941)

Isaiah graphically demonstrates that we cannot be in the presence of the Living God and not be deeply changed to the core. It is in this relationship with God that the soul is brought to an overwhelming height of joy while experiencing a sweet crushing reverence for the one from whom this indescribable love freely, graciously, and generously is lavished: 'Elohiym.

It is here in my individual relationship with a communal God that I am known deeply and loved thoroughly, sin and all. It is only here that I can see who I truly am; a sinner without condemnation (Romans 8:1) and a holy, victorious child of God. It is here that I meet the kingdom. It is here that the kingdom invades all of me; flesh and spirit and transforms me (Philippians 3:21).

SOME GUIDING PRINCIPLES TO PRACTICING THE PRESENCE

Unlike Isaiah, most of us do not have the experience of being transported into the presence of God. Practicing the presence of God is the choice to orient our entire heart, mind, and soul into the reality God's presence. As it is practiced and worked at, the capacity to remain in His presence strengthens and is self-reinforcing. When we go to work, we orient our entire self to the process of work; when we come home, we orient our heart, mind, and soul toward laundry, dinner, homework, and family. Practicing the presence of God is orienting at our awareness to the reality of the Kingdom of God in the here and now.

Dear, sweet, humble Brother Lawrence knew this place. In the early 1600s, he was a monk in a Carmelite monastery. He wrote some letters about staying present with God in all that we do. These letters were later compiled into a book entitled *Practicing the Presence of God.* This very humble monk leveraged the difficulties and simplicities of life to orient toward the reality of God's sovereign rule in his life. Quite unintentionally these letters written by him were left for us.

Knowing that we are easily distractable by nature, it is helpful to enter this practice mindfully and aware that there are many rabbit trails, to–do lists, road bumps, and worries that will demand our attention. What follows are a few things to keep in mind about the practice of presence. This is not an exhaustive list; it is a place to start.

Noticing Anxiety

Misunderstood, anxiety has become something we "got" as opposed to it being a part of every breath. If we can understand anxiety, we can manage and make sense of it. In the last several decades, neuroscience has exploded our understanding of how we work as humans. Neuroscience explains that every thought we have begins in our limbic system, our emotional brain. I am going to introduce the very basics of brain structure. This is so basic that one Google search would tell you a vast amount of more information. I am using this simplicity to make a plain point. The three parts of the brain I would like to introduce you to are the reptilian brain (RB), the limbic system or emotional brain, and the prefrontal cortex, the thinking brain.

The reptilian brain is the brain we are born with. It performs basic life functions inclusive of crying, breathing, defecating, urinating, and sucking. Shortly after we are born, our limbic system starts to develop. For the next several years, the limbic system (emotional brain) is growing. This gives some insight into the emotional level of our young ones. Then roughly between three to six years of age, the prefrontal cortex (thinking brain) begins developing more prominently and continues to grow into the mid-twenties. (There is no linear line of development. These are approximations.)

This is important to our understanding of anxiety because it is our limbic system/emotional brain that is the starting point for all data that is processed. The specific starting point is the amygdala, which is one part of the larger limbic system. One of the amygdala's jobs is to discern whether each piece of data is a danger or not.

To illustrate this, a common story is as follows. If you are walking down a road and see a stick in the middle of it, your amygdala looks at the stick and asks if it is in danger. Is it a snake? Is it a stick? This happens so rapidly that we do not have conscious awareness of the process. Quicker than you can notice, the amygdala searches the hippocampus (library of images) and determines that the item in front of you is a stick and not a snake. You are not in danger. This is a prime example of how every piece of data is oriented first through our anxious center. This is clearly designed to keep us safe in a dangerous world.

The good news is we do not have to be held captive by this process. As Paul writes, "We are destroying arguments and all arrogance raised against the knowledge of God, and we are taking every thought captive to the obedience of Christ" (2 Corinthians 10:5). We could translate the last sentence to "taking every thought captive to the goodness of Christ." We can stop the process of anxiety when we practice grabbing thoughts and bringing them into the goodness of the kingdom.

One day my husband and I were in the midst of an extraordinarily difficult situation that appeared to have no desirable outcome. We talked for hours about how to behave properly in the midst of this potentially catastrophic family conflict. Both of us were experiencing high emotional stress. Our amygdalas were in full operation sending stress hormones all throughout our systems. Alarm bells were ringing, fear was high, anxiety was through the roof. After the exhaustion of the conversation, we both fell silent and distracted. I blurted out, "Hey, John?"

"Yeah," was his response.

"God is in me, right?" I asked.

"Yeah," was his response.

"God is in you, right?" I continued my inquiry.

"Yeah."

"Then this has to work out for the good in the long run," I concluded.

"Yeah, that is right," he said.

There it was. Anxiety reduced. It was reduced, not over. There was grief to process, hurt to heal from, behavior to manage, hearts to keep aligned. One of the things we cling to as a family is that God is good, and all things work out for the good. In no way do we believe that all things are good. There is no one who would say that what we were going through was good, but now, six years later, I can honestly say it did work out for our good. I am truly grateful for that event.

I am fond of saying to clients, "If you're breathing, you're anxious." At brain–circuitry level, that is fundamentally true. So, it is not about "not being" anxious. It is about managing your anxiety.

The belief that God is good and that all things work out for the good is not one I choose to believe or that I give mental assent to. It has been practiced and experienced through my half-century on this planet. It has proven true over and over again. I know it in my bones. Remember that quote attributed to Papua New Guinea's Asaro Tribe I mentioned earlier: "Knowledge is only rumor until it lives in the bones." I know in my bones that God is good and that all things work for the good. This is the work of practicing the kingdom reality in an earthly context.

Given the above, it makes sense that the most common admonition in the Bible is against fear: "No need to be afraid, I have you." "Don't be afraid, I am right here, and I am not going anywhere." The nature of its repetition suggests something. Knowing our frame and that we are but dust (Psalm 103:14), God reminds us who He is, where He is, and what that means for us. When my children were little, they would stand on the side of the pool and struggle to jump in the water when I had my arms outstretched only inches from theirs. I would say, "Don't be afraid. I will catch you." They still struggled mightily. Then I would say, "Have I ever dropped you?" Still, they struggled. They learned trust. They learned that I had their goodness in mind. They learned to override their anxiety through learned trust and the love of their mother.

Tolerating the Tension

Trusting that God is good and that all things work to the good is loaded with tension. Tension, while essential in all relationships, causes us great difficulty due to its very uncomfortable nature. Our bodies respond quickly in the presence of tension. We are compelled to move either toward the tension to resolve it or away to avoid it. Again if it is a snake, I am going to move away from it. If it is a stick, I will move it out of my path.

Quickly responding to tension without consideration and discernment is called reactivity. We are pulled into tension in our efforts to "fix" the problem and then get overwhelmed when the "fix" does not work so we end up moving out because it is too hard to tolerate.

Marriages will inevitably experience tension between two very different beings. It is very true that most folks try quite hard to fix the problems in their marriage; however, unresolved tension carried for years takes a heavy toll and can lead marriages to go silent or volatile.

This storyline is no different in most of our relationships: family, friends, co-workers, church members, neighbors. Our relationship with God is not immune from this tension—all of these relationships are subject to the effects of tension. This tension holds within itself opportunity for destruction or for extraordinary life and healing.

Growth patterns, by design, require tension. Tension is an indicator of needed change. Tension identifies when something is no longer sufficient and there is a need for change in the status quo. As the saying goes, "The only thing in life that doesn't change is change." Tension is both an obstacle to our walk with God and an indispensable part of our maturity into the likeness of Christ. Tension occurs when there is awareness of a lack of knowledge. Tension occurs when we want more. Tension is a signal that we are being invited into a new level of maturity. It is here again that we find our enigmatic free will.

While tension is normal and necessary, what we do in tension makes it either an obstacle or an indispensable aid in growth.

The Obstacle of Tension

The trap of tension is reactivity. Reactivity is when folks make rash decisions against the advice of everyone around them. We can see this when young people get married too quickly or engage in sexual activity too early. These sexual feelings can be overpowering and certainly confusing. If a young person does not know how to work with and in tension, they will often yield to this very powerful bodily drive.

Reactivity is also seen in relationship with God. A strong desire to make a change in life may feel unbearable so it is labeled as "God's call," when it is, in reality, motivated by personal reactivity. We may pray about an issue, and while God might be inviting us into silence and waiting, we label our desires God's and make our own answer. These mistakes are common and fertile soil in which to grow and learn. No judgment. It is a process of learning.

Noticing tension is the hardest part. We often move so quickly to resolve tension that we don't notice what we are actually in the midst of. I have been known on more than one occasion to nail in a screw that got stuck. I couldn't tolerate the unresolved tension so I resolved it. This process of growing in God's way is laden with tension—good and wonderful tension.

> Make me know Your ways, O Lord;
> Teach me Your paths.
> Lead me in Your truth and teach me,
> For You are the God of my salvation;
> For You I wait all the day.
> **Psalm 25:4–5**

Notice in the scripture above: "Make me. . . teach me. . . lead me. . . you are God. . . I wait. . . " Learning requires failure, otherwise it isn't learning, but accomplishment. It is here in tension where we are invited to learn the tenor of His voice as opposed to the desires of our voice. We don't always get it right, but it is here, in tension, that the relationship is built. God not only acknowledges the tension but invites us to work with it.

ENGAGING WITH GOD'S PRESENCE

Depending on the nature of the particular tension, God invites us to pay attention, discern, and engage with this opportunity. He wants to show us the way in and through tension. If the tension is the pull of something unhealthy, resist and move away. In fact, do not go anywhere near it (1 Corinthians 6:18; 1 Thessalonians 5.22). If the tension is that you desire God, He says, "If you come after me with all you have, you will find me" (Jeremiah 29:13). If you want something, ask (Matthew 7:7; James 4:2). Then there is the trickiest part of tension with God, the waiting (Isaiah 40:31, Psalm 27:14). He encourages us to be still and listen (Psalm 45:10; Isaiah 28:23; Psalm 46:10). If during your journey, you are disoriented and do not know what to do, remember, He advises (Isaiah 46:9). Over and over and over again, God called the children of Israel to remember who He is (Deuteronomy 6:12, Exodus 13:3). We are called to remember who He is (1 Chronicles 16:12, Nehemiah 4:14, Psalm 20:7, Psalm 77:11, Isaiah 44:12). Strategies of tolerating tension allow us to be not only present with the work of God in our lives but to also peacefully stay in the tension of others' lives in order to be a heavenly ambassador for the throne. Learning to tolerate the tension is the place of spiritual formation.

Humility

For me, understanding humility has been akin to nailing Jell-O to a wall. Humility is tricky. You can't really see it in folks because it doesn't tend to show up and make a fuss. The only thing I have seen labeled *humility* was the exact opposite. What is labeled *humility* is often just the false self needing desperately to serve the distorted self's need to have others see their righteousness. Richard Foster (1992) with the help of Anthony Bloom actually nailed the Jell-O to the wall.

> "Humility is filled with power to bring forth life. The word itself comes from the Latin *humus*, which means fertile ground. "Humility," writes Anthony Bloom, "is the situation of the earth." In one sense humility is nothing more than staying close to the earth. The earth, Bloom reminds us, is always with us, always taken for granted, always walked on by everyone. It is the place where we dump our garbage. "It's there silent and accepting everything and in a miraculous way making out of all the refuse new richness. . . transforming corruption itself into a power of life and a new possibility of creativeness, open to sunshine, open to the rain, ready to receive any seed we sow and capable of bringing thirtyfold, sixtyfold, a hundredfold out of every seed. Such is the power of humility." (Foster, *Prayer,* 1992)

Richard Foster, with some help from Bloom, nailed it as he has so many other concepts: he defined humility. Accepting without judgment and with confident knowledge, the true self observes and engages as it can without any need to control anyone or anything. The true self is secure in the knowledge that it is in the safest place it could possibly ever be—the hands of the One True Living God. Humility is receptivity; receiving the path God has set before us without manipulation, as the psalmist wrote, "He leads the humble in what is right, and teaches the humble his way" (Psalm 25:9).

Humility is not a call to be a doormat, but a call to live in the Kingdom of God under the tutelage of the King of Kings and the Lord of Lords. We are invited to interact with what He has brought before us—good, bad, blessings, challenges, difficulty—and learn. I have been blessed to work with many talented students in my office as interns and then as graduates working toward licensure. There are those students who believe they know all there is to know and are biding their time. Then there are those students who position themselves to learn and soak up all the knowledge they don't know they don't have but are eager to learn. These latter students were confident, assured, talented and humble. It is their humility that will drive them to excel in their field because of how they position themselves.

Matthew 18:4 Whosoever therefore shall humble himself as this little child, the same is greatest in the kingdom of Heaven.

A humble individual is like a child loaded with endless questions and wanting to understand, touch, taste, and learn. An internship with the God that created the world? I'm in!

> Think of yourselves the way Christ Jesus thought of himself. He had equal status with God but didn't think so much of himself that he had to cling to the advantages of that status no matter what. Not at all. When the time came, he set aside the privileges of deity and took on the status of a slave, became human! Having become human, he stayed human. It was an incredibly humbling process. He didn't claim special privileges. Instead, he lived a selfless, obedient life and then died a selfless, obedient death—and the worst kind of death at that—a crucifixion.
> **Philippians 2:5–8**

Jesus' humility led to the salvation of mankind, "transforming corruption itself into a power of life. . . Such is the power of humility" (Foster, *Prayer*, 1992).

Enjoying Obedience

Obedience has been a huge road bump for me. It is a heavy word. It had caused me to recoil for years. I couldn't figure out why it was a struggle. I love Jesus. I deeply desire to be in communion with the divine Trinity. Obedience throughout my life had been experienced not as a loving protective measure but a means to control and dominate.

Ironically, parenting shifted my soul's perspective on obedience. I am now in a position of requiring obedience. I was very uncomfortable with this reality. However, in my being, I knew that my little boy had to hold my hand as we crossed the street. This was not up for debate. Quite a few things, I discovered, were not up for debate as I protected and cared for this very small human. These were topics for conversations but not negotiations.

Obedience is often portrayed as something Jesus demands. This language suggests an angry, rigid relationship, a relationship organized around domination. Could we work from a different paradigm and say that while He requires obedience, His heart desires obedience for our good? I am offering the idea that Jesus wants obedience *for* us. God does not need our obedience; we need our obedience. I want my child to look both ways before she crosses the street not because I am an austere mom who demands obedience. I expect her obedience for her safety and protection. Let us get plain about this. Sins such as anger, gluttony, malice, hatred, drunkenness, lying, and stealing ultimately lead to bad results. One of the ways to understand the word *sin*, and it is a big word with many ways to understand it, is to miss the mark. Sin can mean not God's best. Sin can mean disobedience, meaning the opposite of the thing God desires for our good. If obedience is practicing the things that are good for us, then we know obedience is not automatic. Obedience is training for the good.

Deconstructing the word *obedience* is challenging, and we want to be careful to not reduce the word to a nice idea. It is a powerful and important word. As mental health clinicians, we must deal with many hard things, such as reporting child abuse or neglect, identifying painful diagnoses, naming addictions, to name a few. While these things are hard and rigid in some ways, if we come at them with gentleness and compassion and understanding, they become more tolerable and doable. In fact, in some cases if we come at them gently, they become opportunities to heal and grow. I have seen people take these opportunities and make life–altering change and I have seen people react rigidly to them and cause more damage.

If we can come at obedience as not a rigid thing but an opportunity to adapt to a loving creator's boundaries, I wonder what might shift in us. If we come at the reality that we will never do obedience perfectly nor does God anticipate that, we can see opportunities to practice obedience and opportunities to grow into obedience. When I became a mental health clinician, I really struggled with what I perceived as stupid constraints on the profession. Now several decades in, I see how these constraints, while not perfect, are there to protect both clinician and client. Similarly, my child doesn't understand why he can't just run across the road and pick up his toy; my constraints feel stupid and unfair to him.

A concluding word on this topic of obedience. We often approach obedience and many other "character changes" through the vehicle of willpower. I believe willpower can work in the short term and in brief spurts. I think of willpower as a match. A lighted match will not keep you warm, but if you have organized a pile of burning material in such a way, a match can be very useful. This is similar to willpower. If you rely solely on willpower, you will be very cold. Neurologically, the reason willpower does not work is that it is primarily a left–brain, logical operation. Our brain is not wired to make character decisions out of our left brain. We make character decisions out of understanding of our identity and that is a right–brain activity. Our identity is primarily formed through relationship. This is why obedience takes time and must be seen in other people and understood in the context of relationship (Coursey, *Transforming Fellowship*, 2016). Our right brain is complicated but in simple terms, it is organized around development through relationship. This makes sense why I began to see and learn about obedience differently because I was working through my relationship with my children. I can now understand that I want to obey Jesus and, of course, I do it poorly. But I want to obey Jesus because I know it is for my good. I trust that.

> The obedient life is one in which we listen with great attention to God's Spirit within and among us. The great news of God's revelation is not simply that God exists, but also that God is actively present. Our God is a God who cares, heals, guides, directs, challenges, confronts, corrects, and forms us. To be obedient means to be constantly attentive to this active presence and to allow God, who is only love, to be the source as well as the goal of all we think, say, and do. (Nouwen, *Spiritual Direction,* 2006)

Leaning out of Legalism

Legalism is a trap that will probably always be with us this side of the veil. We have a proclivity as humans to lean into legalism. I think we lean that way because we are always trying to control circumstances that need to be discerned and developed. If we make rules, it is just a lot easier. The following are a few examples of how we can fall into legalism and how to think differently moving from legalism to grace and truth.

"You are not right with God until you confess your sins."

Thanks be to God that the only thing that makes us right with Him is the blood of Jesus. Confession is not about the act but the process that occurs in you and within the other person to whom we have shared the truth. I am not a theologian; I am a systemic–relationship person. Confession is about being honest and open and taking responsibility in the context of a spiritually mature relationship. Confession is not magical.

Confession is intended to bind us into relationship with one another so that we may grow together in Him. Our confession has the capacity to heal not only us but someone else. On some level what I do for a living is an endless stream of confessions. It is not an uncommon experience for me to be convicted on something in my life as a client is sharing their pain.

> Brothers and sisters, even if a person is caught in any wrongdoing, you who are spiritual are to restore such a person in a spirit of gentleness; *each one* looking to yourself, so that you are not tempted as well. Bear one another's burdens, and thereby fulfill the law of Christ.
> **Galatians 6:1–3**

Confessing is about healing self and one another. As mentioned above, neurologically, we actually need people who are more mature than we are in order to heal. Our brain is not wired to do this outside of community. Our brain is wired to heal and mature through relationship with someone we can see. As the saying goes, it's not taught; it's caught. The saying is neurologically accurate. This is the reason we organize education with internships, apprenticeships, and residencies. We must see it in someone else to truly get it.

Confession with a "spiritual" person is an opportunity to see a reflection of God's love in their being for you. We experience in small glimpses God's love for us as we are with people who love us and hold our sins with compassion and grace. Confession reveals the toxic lies of the distorted self and false self in the context of the loving embrace of a Father who is delighted to be with you wherever you are—no matter your sin (Luke 15:11–32). Confession is an invitation to release the distortions and strengthen the true self, all while deep in the embracing pool of God's grace, where He is delighted, pleased, and ready to forgive and heal. This is His transformational presence.

"Work out your salvation with fear and trembling."

Again, praise be to our great God that our salvation is not up to us but was resolved at the cross. When this sentence is taken out of context, it strips us of the mighty work of God with which we are graciously allowed to cooperate.

> So then, my beloved, just as you have always obeyed, not as in my presence only, but now much more in my absence, work out your salvation with fear and trembling; for it is God who is at work in you, both to will and to work for His good pleasure.
> **Philippians 2:12–13**

Paul is exhorting these folks to do what they have always done and obey the work that God is doing in them. Paul is encouraging folks to listen to God, get present with Him, and cooperate with the work of the Holy Spirit. Paul is encouraging people to continue to work hard—stay in the game and stay engaged. This is important work—take it seriously and work hard at it. But in the end, know it is God who is doing the work.

"God is angry at you for sinning."

Where is that written? I suppose an argument can be made in the Old Testament about His anger with Israel. Was He angry at their sin or was He angry at their refusal to not sin? It appears clear that ancient Israel was deliberate and desirous of sinning. God was not angry with a slip or a regular struggle. He was angry at hearts that didn't want to be with Him but wanted to be with other gods. Wasn't He also patient with Israel for hundreds of years, again and again? Didn't He send message after message after message? Didn't He plead with them? Didn't they kill the messengers He sent, including Himself, in the end? We have contorted God to be a character not unlike the Greek gods. We have contorted God to be capricious, reactive, retaliatory, and frankly impatient.

Is He angry at you, His beloved, when you sin? I propose the answer is no. In fact, I offer that more likely His heart hurts, and He is oriented around the desire to help you work it out of your life. There is no doubt that God hates sin. I hate pornography. I hate gambling. I hate strip clubs. I hate gossip. I hate jealousy. I hate addiction. I hate adultery. I hate violence. I hate these things. I hate when people I love and worship with fall prey to these things. I hate that a lot. Am I mad at them? No. All I have is compassion because of how hard it is to fight against these horrid things. I hate these things because they harm people that God loves and I love. I hate these things because it harms relationships. All sin harms relationship. God is a God of relationship and sin does nothing but muddy that up. He certainly understands it and wants to work with us on removing sin.

The message that God is an angry God is a pernicious lie. He is a just and righteous God.

> "Do not be deceived, God is not mocked; for whatever a person sows, this he will also reap. For the one who sows to his own flesh will reap destruction from the flesh, but the one who sows to the Spirit will reap eternal life from the Spirit.
> **Galatians 6:7–8**

Again, in context, He is a God who will cooperate with what your free will chooses. Notice the intention of "sowing." It's describing the intention to do evil, not the act of making mistakes and coming back with confession. This is a heart issue. An angry God is a precarious God who is quick to judge the slightest infraction, not a God who would go and has gone to extraordinary lengths to beckon those He deeply loves. He has proven over and over again that He is an intimate God with unbounded grace. I would suggest that this angry–God image is likely a byproduct of our fears and not of the living breathing word of God.

The Old Testament is where most folks get the message that God is angry. Remember the Old Testament is actually a rather short story considering the time lapse of the pages. It might appear that God is an angry God, but might I suggest that the timeline actually portrays a very patient, loving, and entreating God desirous of relationship with mankind? We judge God as an angry God when after several hundred years of intolerable and unbearable acts by His people, which violated each other and His Holiness, He disciplines them. This doesn't sound like an angry God but a long–suffering and just God. I might further suggest that God patiently tolerating unspeakable atrocities is always indicative of His desire to turn His people back to Him.

The anger of God is present when man intentionally harms or prevents restoration of another man's heart to God's heart. Jesus was angry with the Pharisees at the temple because they were intentionally taking advantage of folks who were trying to be reconciled to God (Matthew 21:12–13). The Pharisees were profiting from access to God. God's anger was ignited because of abuse. These obscenities hurt other people and prevented true loving relationship with God (Deuteronomy 23:18)—all to line their own pockets.

The message that God is angry is the same message as the serpent's whispers: *You are not truly safe with this God. Protect yourself. Sew some leaves together* (false self) *and hide your nakedness* (distorted self) *because that is shameful. Prior to this nakedness* (true self) *was delightful.*

Just like Adam and Eve in the garden, God tells us that if we choose relationship with Him, this life is the easy yoke with freedom and power. We do not believe Him, just like in the garden. We can do it ourselves and we take that nibble. This all leads to a life burdened (the curse) by dos and do nots. We end up white-knuckling the right and wrong only to be disappointed and self-condemned. We sing the songs, we say the words, but the reality is that we are not living in the power of Christ but are hiding, draped in leaves, cowering in fear of this very angry, unsafe, untrustworthy God. We look like the world because we live like the world—organized around fear.

Do as You Can, Not as You Can't

My dear friend Jan Johnson, author, spiritual director, and very fun person, borrowed from the title of *Pray as You Can, Not as You Can't* by Dom John Chapman and adapted the phrase to encourage folks in their journey of formation. She shares that in the process of this work it can be helpful to practice Do as You Can, Not as You Can't. It is simple in tenor and allows us to be right where we are in our development on this circuitous and at times tedious journey. It encourages us to not move into an area we are not ready for yet. It invites us into our capacity. It invites a crawling baby to stand, not to run.

Power of the Ask in the Now

When asked to name one word that described Jesus, Dallas Willard used *unhurried*. Jesus lived in the now. Demonstrative of this nature, at his rising, the apex of the story of God and man, He took a moment and folded His head napkin (John 20:7). There are no emergency sessions in heaven. No hurry. No little red phone. The Gospels present a Jesus unhurried by the anxiety of life and folks around him; Jesus lived in the now.

In the middle of a pressing, hurried crowd, Jesus paused to make note of a moment that would have gone unnoticed. "Who touched me?" (Mark 5). Jesus grabbed the unhurried now amidst the pressing flesh all around. Jesus took the time to acknowledge the healing of this suffering woman. A woman who was bleeding was unclean. He took the present moment and highlighted this unclean woman as having remarkable faith. Only a couple verses later, Jesus paused again in the middle of His speaking as He overheard a conversation about a little girl who died. As the text reads, He took the present moment and turned. He then left to go to the little girl and entered the home asking, "Why make a commotion and weep?" The question was not a question but the grabbing of the present moment and bringing others into the present–moment reality to reveal a different reality. I think it is okay to say that the question was a setup (Mark 5).

During storms, physical, emotional, or spiritual, there is a simple ask: "What's true?" This ask allows us to see above our current circumstances—above our storm. This simple ask reminds us of what God tells us repeatedly, reminiscent of the disciples in the boat in the storm (Matthew 8). Afraid they were going to die, they woke Jesus. He said, "Why are you afraid, you men of little faith?" Isn't He, in different terms, asking, "What do you know is true?" "What's true?" rises above the details of the storm and asks the important question. In the most brutal of storms, there seems to be a constant truth. God is good, He never leaves us, and all things He uses for our good (Romans 8). It does not say all things are good; it says all things are used for our good. "What's true?" is a good ask. It may still be a nasty, brutal, and lengthy storm. What does this truth change about how you are in the storm?

Jesus, unhurried and in the moment, certainly aware of the people around Him and their hunger and exhaustion, asked, "How many loaves do you have?" (Matthew 15:32–38). The power of the ask is an orienting question. It brought the disciples away from a complaining place to a place of teaching. Their anxiety was high because they knew there was not enough food; the ask repositioned them to learn. The ask teaches the student. The ask invites relationship.

It's a Process

Engaging in the process is an organically unfolding, curious way of engaging with life in the now. Humility, Leaning out of Legalism, Enjoying Obedience, Doing as You Can, Not as You Can't, and The Power of the Ask in the Now are just principles to assist us to stay present in the now with the teacher so that we can learn from the teacher. Learning can only be done in the now as it is occurring. Even if we are pondering the past, we are learning now. The process is about what is going on now, what is unfolding now, what is emerging now. It is an invitation to be in the unhurried presence with Jesus in the now. This is probably the single most undeveloped skill of our time.

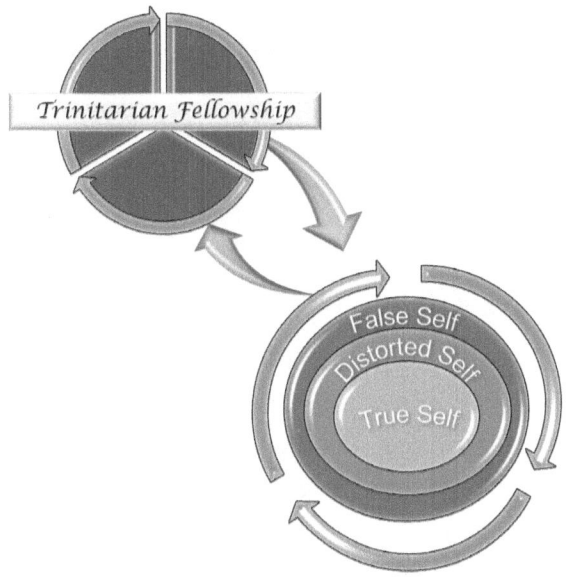

The concepts above are only a starting point, ways to engage with God as He does the work that He so desires to do. It is the reason we are here. The reason He came. The reason He will come again. Being with us is the point. Ways to be with God are limitless and have been practiced through man's entire walk with God.

CHAPTER 8

The Transformative Power of Spiritual Disciplines

Etched in our essence and held in our collective unconsciousness, God is drawing us into relationship with Him and a community of believers. The fabric of this story permeates the story of mankind and our response to this great other.

While the concept of the great other has taken many shapes through many cultures, this great other continuously emerges in our story as we wrestle with the knowledge that there is more. In the early part of the twenty-first century, the term "being spiritual" is quite the fashionable ego accessory. "I am not religious. I am a very spiritual person," is how the phrase goes.

> Spiritual formation, without regard to any specifically religious context or tradition, is the process by which the human spirit or will is given a definite form or character. It is a process that happens to everyone. The most despicable as well as the most admirable of persons have a spiritual formation. Terrorists as well as saints are the outcome of spiritual formation. Their spirits or hearts have been formed. (Willard, *Renovation of the Heart,* 2011)

Spiritual formation is simply the shaping of our spiritual nature, whether it is shaped by art, music, violence, hate, trauma, or Buddhism. Spiritual formation is occurring to every human being that is breathing or has taken a breath. We are spiritual beings; it is happening. As Dallas Willard humorously stated, "The rocket of our life is off the pad. Action is forever. We are becoming who we will be—forever."

American spiritual formation is most commonly left to the drifting inclination of culture. Much like water that slowly carves out massive riverbeds, the mass flow of current ideas shapes our spirit without any considered thought. Being a good person is surely the right answer. Random acts of kindness are a popular trend. Just as randomly going to the gym does not develop optimum health, neither does randomly tending to our spiritual nature develop spiritual maturity. Random does not shape anything; random quells the nagging whisper and leaves our spiritual formation to the slow inevitable shaping of culture and trends.

Without considerable attention, the prevailing wind has replaced discernment, thoughtful dialogue, and meaningful commitment. This is as true in our culture as it can be in our churches. It is easier to receive what is handed over for consumption than to discern truth. Not attending to our spiritual formation allows for the trends of popular and passing phases to shape our souls without thought. The depth of our belief is revealed with the changing wind.

Will we take the reins of our spiritual formation, or will we let it just happen? Compare a person born in the palaces of Europe to a soul born in the streets of Bangladesh; two very different souls formed. Not solely destined to be what birth circumstances prescribe, free will ensures an individual's capacity to be deliberate about exposure, input, and integration. A quick answer to the question of the fate of the two souls born in these two different places suggest a certain trajectory for their lives. All very plausible, but not the only possibility. Free will is a persnickety reality. Free will makes us responsible. Whether we hand our free will over to the driving trends of our culture or the pastor of our church, or we choose to yield to the truth of our Creator, a decision has been made.

CHRISTIAN SPIRITUAL FORMATION

Christian spiritual formation is an intentional choice to organize our life in such a way as to be present with God and interact with the transforming work of the Holy Spirit as we are transformed into the image of Christ.

> The consistent practice of spiritual disciplines marked Jesus' life. Prayer, solitude, fasting, meditation, worship, and service were part of His fabric of life. They are critical because they place us in God's healing and sustaining presence. They also contain physical, psychological, social, intellectual, and emotional dimensions. The proper grace–oriented practice of these disciplines is an essential part of our formation, moving us from reliance on our own willpower to dependence on God's grace. Spiritual disciplines in themselves can do very little by way of spiritual change, but when we use them to place us in God's presence, God can do His loving, restorative work. (Wilhoit, *Spiritual Formation,* 2008)

This transformation into the measure of the stature which belongs to the fullness of Christ is the work of the Holy Spirit. Our active participation is required (Ephesians 4:11–13).

> Discipleship, however, calls for discipline. Indeed, discipleship and discipline share the same linguistic root (from the Latin *discere*, which means "to learn from"), and the two should never be separated. Whereas discipline without discipleship leads to rigid formalism, discipleship without discipline ends in sentimental romanticism. It requires an enormous human

effort to be and to stay in the world with it many demands while keeping our hearts and minds solidly anchored in God. The various disciplines of the spiritual life are meant for freedom and are [a] reliable means for the creation of helpful boundaries in our lives within which God's voice can be heard, God's presence felt, and God's guidance experienced. Without such boundaries that make space for God, our lives quickly narrow down; we hear and see less and less, we become spiritually sick, and we become one-dimensional, and sometimes delusional, people. The only remedy for this is the intentional practice of prayer and meditation (Nouwen, *Spiritual Formation,* 2010).

Centuries old and practiced by our spiritual mothers and fathers, the disciplines are a beautiful heritage of those who have walked before us. St. Paul, St. Francis of Assisi, Julian of Norwich, Theresa of Avila, Joan of Arc, Bernard of Clairvaux, and so many more have engaged the disciplines as a way of setting their mind on the things above (Colossians 3:2) and aligning their spirits to heaven. Time–tested, well–traveled, and enduring practices, the disciplines are designed to orient the soul, mind, and body into the presence of the Almighty God.

Spiritual formation, because it is occurring regardless of effort, demands a question: "What is forming our essential spiritual nature?" Are we going to choose our formation, or will our formation be chosen for us? Exhortation from scripture remind us to teach our children as we go (Deuteronomy 6), think on things that are good (Philippians 4), and Paul's exhortation to be imitators of me (I Corinthians 4), reminds us that we must choose our orientation. Left unattended our flesh and its strong pulls will choose our orientation. The flesh will always choose pleasure; it is not designed to choose the things of heaven; it is designed to be drawn toward dazzling bobbles and pleasing stimulus. Christian spiritual formation is the conscious, intentional choice to orient our entire selves toward the things of God.

A Mind Set On

As Paul reminds us, "Set your mind on the things above, not on the things that are on earth" (Colossians 3:2).

Relationships require a choice to be mindful. When my kids were toddlers, they would often have a story of a great injustice to tell. So, when tugged at by a small one, I would set my mind on their reality. I would descend from my lofty 5'6" altitude to their 2'5" reality to meet them face to face, wipe away a tear, and get into this moment of perceived trauma in order to hear the lengthy, complicated explanation of the disastrous event that just occurred over at the train table with brother. What a joy to be in their world for a moment.

In pursuit of learning more about my husband in our first years of marriage, I became a football fan. I didn't want to do this, but I chose to orient my entire being in front of that football game to be present with this man that I loved. Never having watched a game in full, ever, I became a fan and have been known to get a bit excited now and again.

Relationship requires orientation. We must physically be oriented toward the folks whom we love in order to build relationship. In both of these accounts, I moved away from my fleshly orientation of what I wanted to do and oriented myself toward another for sake of relationship, which is the essence of kingdom living—relationship with God, self, and one another.

Rehabilitation of the Flesh

For the mind set on the flesh is death, but the mind set on the Spirit is life and peace, because the mind set on the flesh is hostile toward God; for it does not subject itself to the law of God, for it is not even able to do so, and those who are in the flesh cannot please God.

Romans 8:6–8

The disciplines are a time–tested training program for kingdom living. When man was made, it appears that God did not say that all of creation was good but fleshly man was bad. Our flesh is not inherently evil but is inherently oriented around meeting needs. This is critically necessary; if our flesh was not oriented around meeting its needs, we wouldn't survive. Our flesh is oriented around breathing. If it were up to me, I probably would forget to breathe. We do not think about it. The reptilian brain is working just fine. It is not selfish to breathe in oxygen. It is not selfish to put food into our mouths. The flesh is just what it is. . . flesh. The truth is that the flesh is not bad but was always designed to work at its optimum under kingdom reality.

The disciplines are activities that orient our entire self toward kingdom reality, where all parts of ourselves work rightly. Culture tells us that freedom is letting the flesh be satiated by desire. The message is that this is true freedom, free of all restraint. This has not proven to be true—as is testified by the history books and a moment of serious cogent thought. True freedom is to be organized rightly, as we were designed—in relationship with God, self, and one another.

Here is the easy yoke and abundant life, where the disciplines set us free to live at peak efficiency, the way we were designed from the beginning. The disciplines orient us into relationship with God and organize our being to run the way it was designed, which illumines our true reality as sons and daughters of the Most High God and sets us free to live as an "unceasing spiritual being with an eternal destiny in God's great universe" (Dallas Willard).

SHAKING LOOSE AND MOVING INWARD

Everyone who drinks of this water will be thirsty again; but whoever drinks of the water that I will give him shall never be thirsty; but the water that I will give him will become in him a fountain of water springing up to eternal life.

John 4:13–14

But an hour is coming, and now is, when the true worshipers
will worship the Father in spirit and truth; for such people
the Father seeks to be His worshipers. God is spirit, and those
who worship Him must worship in spirit and truth.
John 4:23–24

For our dear friend on the mountain beside the well, worship was
about a place. Jesus invited this precious woman into relationship with
Him to worship. She was oriented toward a place without, and Jesus
was inviting her to a place within. Jesus was saying that there is a time
coming when "true worshipers" will not need a "right place." The place
of worship is now between Him and her.

The message on that mountain was not for her alone; it is for us.
The story of mankind is about our insatiable desire to control all things
inclusive of the gift Jesus brought—relationship with God. In the earliest
of our days, we struggled around the requirement of circumcision (Acts
15). Then there was the battle of Gnosticism, Arianism, Docetism, and
many other *isms*. In the early 1500s, we had the issue of who, when, and
how we are to be baptized. These are weighty matters that demand our
considered time and attention. However, we must not neglect weightier
matters of the law (Matthew 23:23). Justice, mercy, and faith are the
weightier matters Jesus named. These weightier matters are all relationship–based.

The struggle continues today. From talking in tongues to worship
music to skirt lengths, we have not changed much. Our personal illu-
sions of Christianity become the dogma we must force upon someone
else in order to reduce our anxiety that we have it "right." This is a life
disempowered of the horsepower of heaven. This is Christianity empow-
ered by doing right, not a life responding to the invitation to worship
Him in spirit and truth.

Shaking loose of formulaic Christianity, this personal invitation reminds us that this process is unique to each of us and our interactivity

with God. It challenges us to pay attention to our anxiety, which leads to legalism—"doing it right" and "putting God in a box" (i.e., God is exactly this way or God is exactly that way). Practicing the disciplines allows God to be God and allows Him to show up as He will as we position ourselves into His presence. Shaking loose of formulaic Christianity, the disciplines are not just another curriculum to replace existing ones. The disciplines are a process, classic in nature and personalized to the individual. This is what makes this process intimate, a unique journey between you and your God as you are set free to be loved, cherished, and nurtured by the power that shaped the universe.

Just as I set my attention on my husband by orienting my entire being on the couch in front of the football game, just as when I set my attention on my dear son and centered on his beautiful curious eyes, I choose as a worshiper of God to orient my mind, body, and soul to the presence of the Almighty God and enjoy the fellowship of the Trinity.

While God is so kind to be always with us, we have only to turn. As we practice turning and choosing God, we develop a habit of turning.

[If] My people who are called by My name humble themselves, and pray and seek My face, and turn from their wicked ways, then I will hear from heaven, and I will forgive their sin and will heal their land.
2 Chronicles 7:14

CHAPTER 9

The Seven Disciplines

There are many ways to organize and present the disciplines. In his classic and important work *Celebration of Discipline: The Path to Spiritual Growth*, Richard Foster organized the disciplines into Inward Disciplines, Outward Disciplines, and Corporate Disciplines. Disciplines of Engagement and Disciplines of Abstinence are how Dallas Willard organizes his presentation in *The Spirit of the Disciplines*. These books are important works to deeply engage with and process.

It is important to note that my treatment of the topic of the disciplines is not intended to be exhaustive. My aim is to present the disciplines in such a way that they are seen as inviting, doable, and non-rigid. My aim is to gently offer a shift from our proclivity as Christians to be legalistic and perfect. My aim is to present the disciplines as a way of growing in joyous, creative relationship with the fabulous Trinity.

THE THREE S'S: SILENCE, SOLITUDE, AND STILLNESS

Due to a screeching halt of all activity and noise, solitude, stillness, and silence (SSS) create space. Space has a tendency to make us uncomfortable. We have become accustomed to busy and full. From nap time, school time, dinner time, summertime, vacation time, we are organized around time. It drives us. In many ways, it is our task master. Go, go, go!

As a result, seeking SSS can be disorienting and challenging. Both the mind and the body will struggle with solitude. In solitude our bodies seek familiar input: a song, an email, a text. We may conquer those small skirmishes, but the real battle is the mind. Invasions of thoughts—phone calls that need to made, bills that need to be paid, dentist appointments to schedule, leaky roofs to fix, and difficult family get-togethers to attend—are insidiously distracting. There are a couple ways to beat these relentless incursions. One is to let them float by. These nagging items tend to come back around again. Treat them like you would birds floating in the air; notice them, but do not follow them. The second way of responding to them is to write them down. Have a piece of paper out of sight but within your reach. Jot the thoughts down and move on.

If it's so challenging, why should we take the time to engage in the three S's?

- Stillness removes agenda and stills our constant movement
- Silence quiets the noise and orients us to His time zone
- Solitude gets us out of other people's agendas and needs and invites us into His invitation to be and know

And while SSS can feel like culture shock, it is our reaction to the culture of heaven, where there is no anxiety, no pressure, no hurry, and no need to fill empty space because all of space is filled with the simple knowledge that God is. SSS invites us into that reality. "Be still and know that I am" (Psalm 46:10 bsb).

So how do we go about it? Most of us cannot take a week off and go away to be with God. Most of us are not called to lead a monastic life.

We must "do as we can, not as we can't."

Our radical solitude might be a day away at a retreat house unencumbered by relationships. It might be thirty minutes alone in His presence. It might be a walk in nature with no intrusion of sound in our ears. For parents of small babies, maybe a morning walk in a quiet park will do. When you are working seventy–hour weeks to just get by, your drive to work without the radio will do. In a house consumed with people and noise, a bath with ear plugs will do.

As life changes, opportunities for more space might arrive. Silence, stillness, and solitude are not just a place to be, but a state of mind. Insomnia is a wonderful place to be still and silent with our spirit oriented to God's presence.

SSS forces us to wrestle with the reality that His main agenda is our being present with Him. He isn't anxious, nor does He have a to–do list for shaping us into the image of Jesus Christ. For someone coming from a Christian culture organized around "being good enough," this concept is truly mind-altering; we can leave behind frantic attempts to be Christlike. It is only shared communal presence with this living, loving God that will allow us to comprehend this truth: He really enjoys our presence.

Let's take a deeper dive into solitude, stillness, and silence.

Solitude

Jesus engaged in this practice of solitude often and taught the disciples to do as well. We see ample evidence of His seeking solitude (Mark 6:31; Matthew 14:3; Luke 5:16). We see Him going into the desert for forty days, His time of solitude preceding His time of ministry. Seeking solitude was not only modeled repeatedly by Jesus but continued in the early church for centuries. Foster (2010-10-12) chronicles this practice as a literal practice to follow:

> "This movement [of desert solitude] cannot be traced to one particular person, though Antony of Egypt was its most famous leader. At the beginning of the fourth century leaders and contemplative communities started settling in the desert—first

in the desert of Nitria (southwest of Alexandria and the Nile Delta) and then in the desert of Scete and area known as 'the Cells.' By the middle of the fourth century Antony's followers and thousands of other ascetics were devoting themselves to prayer and following Christ while living in the desert."

Solitude challenges the clash between our reality and the reality of heaven. Solitude shakes loose perception, agenda, and distortions. Solitude makes full in your soul the reality of the Kingdom of God. As followers of Christ, we are residents of both realities. Solitude is the experience that clarifies and fortifies that which we are servant to.

Last fall, I was reaching burnout. Throughout the year, I have regularly scheduled times for solitude where I retreat to a monastery near me. That was not what I needed. I needed to be free. I had not been free for a long time.

I began by finagling several days in a row without anyone (other than my husband and kids) needing me for anything.

Then I indulged a longtime desire—I bought a double hammock. I did not know what a double hammock was but was quite hopeful that, in addition to providing a reflective space for me, it would be a place for snuggling with a few kiddos.

I soon discovered that the huge hammock was so large it almost cocooned me. I could see none of the houses around me or people or cars on the street. All I could see was the sky and a few trees.

The good news is that I had unexpectedly found solitude. I unexpectedly found God. It was just me and Him. It was delightful as I floated in the breeze, wondering about clouds, and breathing in His gracious, easy presence. Then to my sheer delight, my solitude was broken by a big yellow bus and the delightful squeals of "Mom, can I get in there with you?"

Solitude is more about orientation and presence than it is about being alone. Solitude is the awareness of the fullness and presence of

God occupying every space of our soul. Solitude invites us to move away from Martha distracted by business into a position of Mary sitting at Jesus' feet. "Martha, Martha, you are worried and bothered about so many things; but only one thing is necessary, for Mary has chosen the good part, which shall not be taken away from her" (Luke 10). Jesus was not criticizing the Marthas of this world; they get some serious matters accomplished. It is the Marthas of the world who do not tend to the "only necessary" thing that He is seeking to draw. Mary was so full of Jesus' presence that she was consumed by it. She had found God. It was just her and Him. She was so alone in solitude that she forgot her customary duties. Radical solitude pushes out all cares of the world and invites every crevice to be filled with His presence.

Stillness

Space evokes in us a compelling need to do. Stillness violates this evocation by way of creating not just space but radical space. We can slow down our pace which creates more space between our busy activities. We can "take a breather" by doing a different, maybe even relaxing, activity. However, stillness by its nature creates radically confusing space. Stillness's first enemy is the management of the body's impulsive desire to assert power. To be still requires that we give up the power to act. To be still is to cease from activity.

I was part of a cult for the first twenty-five years of my life. We were Sabbatarians, which meant that we did nothing but study the Bible, eat, and go to church from Friday sundown to Saturday sundown. We could take a walk as long as we did it to enjoy God's nature. We could sing, as long as we sang songs to God. After doing all the approved activities, there was a lot of empty time to fill.

Being born and raised in the practice, it was not foreign but still challenging (Want to mess with a teenager? Force her to do nothing for twenty-four hours).

And yet, despite the challenges, I discovered stillness. For me there was a sense of freedom to just hang with God. Paradoxically defined by time—sundown to sundown—it seemed in a small way that we were free from the burden of the clock. I would never admit this to my friends, but there were times I felt sad the Sabbath was over. I enjoyed the space.

The harder villain of stillness is the mind. A wily creature exhaustively racing from task to task, worrying from fear to fear, seeking endless pleasure, harboring, conjuring, and nurturing every last sinful hope, the mind is in desperate need of taming.

> "Rest in the Lord and wait patiently for Him; Do not fret."
> **Psalm 37:7**

> "Take captive every thought to make it obedient to Christ."
> **2 Corinthians 10:5 (NIV)**

Take captive is right. It requires capturing, for the mind is a clever beast capable of soaring to great heights and equally skilled at plumbing the depths of darkness. Never one for leaving us hanging without some simple guidance, God has some thoughts on the matter. We are invited to "Be still and know that I am." Be still and commune is another invitation (Psalm 4:4).

> Blessed are they that dwell in thy house: they will be still praising thee.
> **Psalm 84:4 (KJV)**

> Wait for the LORD; Be strong and let your heart take courage;
> Yes, wait for the LORD.
> **Psalm 27:14**

God is our help as we attempt to still our minds and focus on His presence.

Silence

The truth is that we can find lasting satisfaction only in the service of that Person who alone can fill the measure of our radical solitude, and who is accessible only in silence.
–Abbot John Eudes Bamburger

My soul, wait in silence for God only, For my hope is from Him.
Psalm 62:5

Reminiscent of Isaiah at the throne, this tenor of God's communication is silence. In silence, Isaiah was convicted. In the silence, he was undone. It is in silence that we engage with our spirit and the Spirit is given. It is here that we listen differently. I imagine the glory and magnitude of the throne room left Isaiah speechless. Might that be what the invitation is? Might the invitation in silence be to wrestle with and work at grasping the magnitude of who God truly is? Might it be an invitation to gaze upon the glory of God? Might it be an invitation to be elevated to the reality of His altitude? Might the invitation in SSS be to rest in His healing presence? God is at work in the silence, as the prophet wrote: "The LORD will fight for you while you keep silent" (Exodus 14:14).

Silence is not in opposition to praying. Silence is a prayer of presence. Silence is worship of adoration. Silence is not the absence of words but the presence of assent. We are so filled with noise in our culture that we have lost the importance and value of silence. When watching a sunset, we instinctually remain silent because He is present in His creation.

SUBMISSION

Abused and misunderstood, submission has, in many cases, become an unholy and onerous slavery robbing it of its truest essential nature. Submission is a free gift of love that can never be demanded or commanded because by virtue of that act it becomes slavery. The corruption of this word has buried a glorious lost way of love. Submission has become a word that instinctually causes revulsion.

To think about this remarkably powerful way of love and in hopes of removing reactivity, I am going to replace the word *submission* with *yielding*. Submission sadly has become burdened with the idea of dominance over another with free will being removed. Yielding is a choice to withhold our power over another in a voluntarily act of giving up our right for the sake of another. I may yield my right of way to another car to prevent a collision or I might yield my right of way as a gift of time. Yielding blesses the one who yields and the one yielded to. Kingdom living is defined by yielding.

Let's take a look at the iconic scripture for submission and replace it with yield.

Husbands and wives, yield one to another out of respect and honor for Christ. Husbands, out of your great love for your wife, yield to Christ, as Christ yielded to the cross out of his great love for the church. Wives, yield to your husbands as he does the challenging work of yielding to Christ. Do this, as you already have done. Husbands, you are called to this same self-sacrificing love for your wife that Christ did for the church. Husbands adore and care for your wives as Christ loves the church and willingly yielded to death on the cross. This is all done by yielding one to another.

UNAUTHORIZED VERSION OF THE BIBLE BY T. MCMORRIS

The husband dies to Christ for the sake of love of his wife, as Christ died to the cross for the sake of love of the church. Paul is instructing in the cycle of submission, a cycle of yielding. Husbands, put your wives first. A husband, concerned with providing an environment where his wife can become glorious, evokes a natural response in a wife. She turns. When she turns toward him, he is strengthened and encouraged and continues to turn toward her. The cycle of submission builds into relationship and strengthens intimacy.

I have worked with countless couples, Christian and non-Christian. Like clockwork and with very few exceptions, when a man turns to serve his wife and puts her first (as Christ did), a wife almost always immediately turns. I often have to point to the turning because the couple has not noticed it. Yielding begets yielding begets yielding begets yielding. It is a wonderful thing to see.

Of course, this process is a bit more challenging when there have been decades of neglect and hurt. Several years ago, the book *Fireproof* by Eric Wilson came out based upon the same principle. Client after client told me I had to watch the movie or read the book. What they didn't know is that I see this principle at work every day in my office, when one person voluntarily yields to another person and there is a turning toward each other.

Years ago, when I started working with couples, I would have folks come sit on my couch, both equally hurt, angry, stuck, and unmoving. (To be clear, the population I am speaking of is generally relatively healthy folks without significant mental instability and without personality disorders.) I was puzzled, wondering who do I ask to move first? I did not know what to do because to ask one person to move before the other is hurtful because it feels like I'm picking sides.

So, I thought I would let them decide. I summarized and validated the hurt that each of them felt, and then I shared my conundrum. Who moves first? Without exception, when one person volunteers, it is always the male. It has yet to prove false. This is not a criticism of women; it is a highlight that men know they are supposed to go first. Instinctually, men are designed to provide and protect. When I ask a husband what his job is in the marriage, again remembering the population I am working with, without exception every man says that his job is to provide and protect without prompting. This is hardwired. They do not get together in secret male meetings and agree on an agenda. They just know it deep in their being. This is their job. Just like in Ephesians, the man goes first. Just like Christ, who went first.

When a husband provides an environment where the wife is safe, cared for, and cherished, the wife responds. He puts her first and yields to her needs, which evokes in a woman a yielding response—the cycle of submission.

Marriage matters are terribly complicated, and it often takes years to untangle all the pain, neglect, hurt, disrespect, and pain.

This is not a book on marriage. It is a book on how the kingdom is built by relationship. The cycle of submission is one piece of a much larger process, but it is significant to the process of relationship work. It is not just in marriage that we can find the cycle of submission.

Looking at scripture through the lens of yielding, we see a new beautiful world of invitation, an invitation to yield in order to be wholly known and deeply loved, an invitation into a community of *yada*. God modeled the relational elements that are the answers to our seeking questions.

> "Teacher, which is the great commandment in the Law?" And He said to him, "'You shall love the Lord your God with all your heart, and with all your soul, and with all your mind.' This is the great and foremost commandment. The second is like it, 'You shall love your neighbor as yourself.' On these two commandments depend the whole Law and the Prophets."
> **Matthew 22:36–40**

Might this be an invitation instead of a demand? Might this be an answer to "how"? How can I be in this community of *yada*? Yield and love are the answer. This is not only what we do but what we experience. He did it first before the foundations of the world.

> "Teacher, what are the governing principles of this community you are inviting us into?" And He said to him, "Yield and Love God with everything you have." This is the core of how things work in this community. The God that consistently yields all He has is the center of this community. The second guiding principle of this community is to yield and release the love you have been so graciously given to others. Everything rests on these truths. (Matthew 22:36–40 from the Unauthorized Version of the Bible by T. McMorris)

This very nature of the kingdom is demonstrated in how the Trinity interrelates. The Holy Trinity demands nothing, only invites and yields. The Father yields attention to the Son, in whom He is well pleased. The Son yields attention from Him to reveal the Father when instructing the disciple to pray. The Son yields His authority and only speaks what the Father would have Him speak. The Father yields His relationship with Jesus to the cross for the sake of me and you. Jesus freely yields His life to the cross for anyone who will call on His name as savior. Then Jesus yields his presence on earth to the presence of the Holy Spirit. The Holy Spirit then yields His action on earth in us by direction of the Father—the cycle of submission.

Jesus yielded to the cross, and because He did this for us and loves us so much, we respond to Him and yield to Him, which evokes a love to serve others. So, we freely yield our time to be in relationship with others who need love. We go and share this love because we are so very loved—the cycle of submission.

Practicing submission is a simple task; it's simply finding ways in a day to release our power for the sake of others. Holding a door open when we are in a hurry. Giving space in a dialogue for another, yielding your need to talk. Yielding to someone the right of way verbally, socially, or physically. Yielding a lane to a car pressing in from behind.

The experiencing of yielding in little things encourages yielding in large ways. "Doing as you can and not as you can't" allows us to work in the little spaces for transformation.

Confession

Confession, a discipline of light, destroys darkness. Struggling in private cripples our capacity to heal and restrains the hand of grace to do its wondrous work. Sins, burdens, fears, and worries held in private are generally laden with distortions and lies masquerading as truth.

Sadly, it is exactly these distortions that keep the issues in the dark and us acting out of the distorted and false self. Lies beget distortions beget lies beget distortions. It is in darkness away from the light of truth, grace, and community that we are free to minimize, excuse, rationalize, and condemn, which further reinforces the need for darkness.

Isolated and living in fear, we are just where the evil one would have us—ripe for the picking. Imprisoned by lies, we have cordoned ourselves off from hope. Einstein rightly said, "No problem can be solved from the same level of consciousness that created it." It is the consciousness of others that can lighten the darkness. It is the holy reflection of a sister in Christ who shares the higher consciousness. Hope for freedom is in truth, grace, and community by way of confession.

Confession is a revelation of truth. As painful as truth may be, at times it is freedom from the darkness of lies that limit and damage relationship with God, self, and one another. Confession destroys isolation. Truth safely shared creates openness and camaraderie, which imparts freedom for all. It is this environment of safety and truth that bids darkness's farewell. Darkness releases truth into the hands of grace, where grace may have its full rendering in the creation of a binding community: relationship with God, self, and one another. Confession binds us one to another in our weaknesses through grace and fortifies our courage to remain. Confession binds us in relationship.

Practicing confession "as you can and not as you can't" might start with apologizing for small offenses. It might be defying the false self pretentiousness and allowing the true self to reveal that there is information that needs to be shared. Confession is working from the true self. Confession is about not hiding. Confession might be a moment to ask the professor to elaborate because you are not getting it. It is risky business, this confession thing. It is always risky business to be acting from the true self that is why the false and distorted self were created.

A word must be said about healthy confession and a healthy confessor. Confession shared with the intent of reinforcing victimhood, producing shame in others, demonstrating righteousness, evoking sympathy for sympathy's sake is not confession but manipulation for self-need, which is sin against a brother. Confessors who seek to know sins to maintain or gain a higher position, use as leverage to spiritually or physically control, or to fulfill their need to dispense their wisdom are not confessors but wolves in sheep's clothing.

Prayer

Shaking loose from the iconic idea of what prayer looks like, but by no means abandoning, allows us to consider that prayer is something much more than a list of requests said in a certain order a couple times a day. Prayer, in very broad terms, is man's engaging in relationship with God to any degree in any way.

Engaging in relationship in the simple can be a nod or wink to a loved one. There is much ado about the disconnection that technology brings. I understand the argument. However, I enjoy technology for the purposes of remaining connected. I may not see a loved one for years who is 3,000 miles away, but I can send a quick hello, joke, or smile to remind them that they are loved. What if we could text God? Who says we can't? Get a post-it note. That'll do. Might you tell God a joke? Why not? He's got quite the sense of humor. What if we engage in prayer nonverbally?

I lived in the Midwest for a good portion of the beginning of my life. The storms in the Midwest are so cool. They can last for more than a day and change in dramatic intensity. I love weather—all of it. One night in my early twenties, I was home alone with my father. We had a challenging relationship. He was a wonderful man of few words. I am a soul of many, many, many, many words. A lightning storm was brewing. I went out on the front porch to watch it. My father joined me. Nothing was said between us but truly it is one of my favorite memories.

I recall driving long distances with my family. When everyone in the van was asleep, I would climb into the front seat and just be with him. Now the smell of coffee in the car while driving at night will bring me to tears quickly as I remember my father. Sharing time—sharing presence is prayer. Prayer is a request of presence. How that presence is spent is wide open to choice.

"Pray as you can, not as you can't."

Prayer might be a picture drawn to share with heaven—offered on the altar of pain. Prayer might be a poem written from the soul of encompassing love. Prayer might be a breathless moment of intoxicating acknowledgment of His glorious creation. Prayer might be a whispered promise because that is all you can hang onto in the midst of the storm. Prayer might be a token you carry as a reminder that you are part of God's aim in all of history, "the creation of an all–inclusive community of loving persons, with Himself included in that community as its prime sustainer and most glorious inhabitant" (Dallas Willard). Prayer is a choice to be present with God.

Many years ago now, my father became ill with an aggressive form of multiple myeloma bone cancer. Once he finally got diagnosed, he was far down the path, mostly because he just lived with the pain; he sort of refused to be sick. He lived only four months after that.

I remember vividly the day I heard the diagnosis. I remember opening my Bible for comfort, and all I can say is that someone took all the words out of my Bible. There were no words on the page. I went to all the comforting places, and the same was true on every page. . . no words. Of course, it was shock. I started to panic. Why couldn't I feel anything? I needed comfort and it was gone. My higher consciousness knew what was going on, but it hurt so badly and I needed something. . . anything.

I closed the Bible, a bit disappointed that the living word of God did not aid me in my grief. I hazily remember going online. I do not know what I was thinking, but I knew I was desperate. I found my childhood friend's photography website and looked around there awhile. She had taken a picture of something and quoted a verse in the picture. There it was.

> You who have been borne by Me from birth
> And have been carried from the womb;
> Even to your old age I will be the same,
> And even to your graying years I will bear you!
> I have done it, and I will carry you;
> And I will bear you and I will deliver you.
> **Isaiah 46:3-4**

It hit me like a shock from a spiritual defibrillator. I proceeded to pillage through the internet and found a beautiful pastoral image of a huge tree at the edge of a field at dawn. I put this scripture on the image and saved it as a picture. For a woman of many words, I had no words. I just had pain. I could not much pray. I could not much do anything normal with God. I was not angry too terribly much, mostly just overwhelmed with pain and sadness.

Over the next several months, my precious and close journey with my Father in heaven was marked mostly by images. This image became my first lifeline. I clung to it like I would cling to my father's leg as a little girl when I was scared. I did not pray the words; I prayed the image. During the quick decline of my father, my personal, deeply painful, and grieving prayers were prayers of images. There were times that my prayers were verbal but during the crushing pain and tears, it was just images. It was all I had.

> To pray, I think, does not mean to think about God in contrast to thinking about other things, or to spend time with God instead of spending time with other people. Rather, it means to think and live in the presence of God. (Beumer, *Henri Nouwen,* 1998)

I reflect on that journey with my God who was so very close with fondness and warmth in the midst of agonizing pain. From a conservative rigid Christian background, the discipline of prayer looked really just one way: on your knees, head bowed, hands folded, and prayer list in hand. The discipline of prayer is so elemental to the walk of any Christian. Does it need to be only one way, or does prayer reflect our individual relationship with God? I know I talk to my kids in lots of different ways. We sing. We giggle. We tickle. We hold hands. We snuggle. We cry. We eat. We talk. We play. We walk. We fight. We leave notes. We give gifts. We paint pictures. We sometimes paint each other.

Prayer is doing relationship with God—no matter what that looks like.

SERVICE

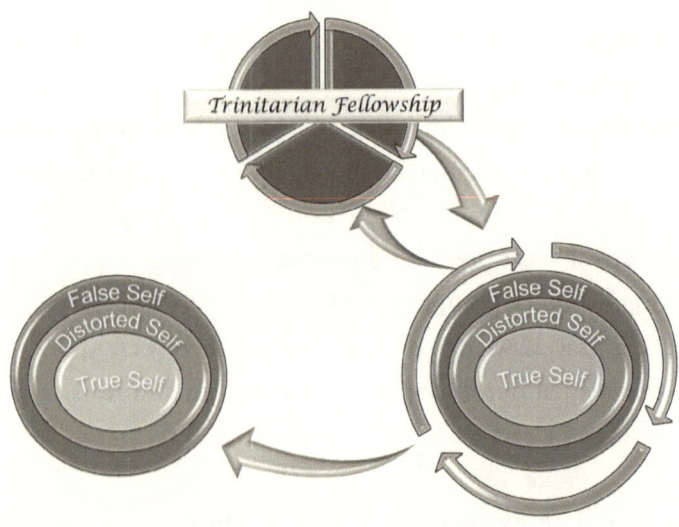

Holy boots on hard ground—service is an insurgence of good in a land of evil. The territory to be overrun is not just the mission fields out there but also the mission fields in front of us. Service overtly violates the instinctual drive to meet our own needs and redirects our physical activities to the kingdom consciousness. Advancing the kingdom in efforts of love, service challenges our myopic state and shakes loose our narrow parameters and perspectives. Service, like nothing else, will change a soul forever.

I had the privilege for a time to become friends with a beautiful woman in the inner city of Syracuse, New York. I drove her to the store because there was no way to get to a grocery store without a car—with the exception of purchasing food at the corner store which has outrageous prices and unhealthy food. I listened to her story. I told her mine. We laughed together. We shared meals together. We cooked together. We talked about being on public assistance and how impossible it felt to disentangle. We strategized. We plotted, really. She reached out to comfort me during the death of my father. I will never forget that phone call.

She is wonderful and remains a piece of my heart. I was forever changed by her and her story. I shared her world for a time; it was a hard world. Her courage and love for Jesus were inspiring. Intense life events separated our worlds as so often is the case with people who cross our paths. We can't change the entirety of the world, but we can love the world in front of us. I loved her. She loved me. She changed me. Sisters forever. Service provides the opportunity to experience someone else's world and for a time to share their yoke, a beautiful incarnation. This relationship produced compassion, understanding, and grace, the aroma of God.

Love is defined here as our choice to orient our will for the good of another. Service is actionable love. The action of the kingdom is advancing efforts of love where only good can overcome evil.

> Service of one another is the nature of the kingdom, Darrell Johnson explains: "Yes, at the center of the universe is servanthood. The Father serves the Son. The Son serves the Father. And that Servanthood is so real it eternally manifests itself as the Spirit of servanthood. The circle is the circle of servanthood." (*Conversations*, Spring/Summer 2015)

Service as a state of mind in the now is how we cooperate with the work of the kingdom. The person who crosses your path is your mission field, as you might be theirs. Working in the moment from a position of service allows for a soul to come in contact with God's divine grace by way of you. A moment to touch, a moment to listen, a moment to hear, a moment to grieve, a moment to giggle—these are all moments to serve as God with skin on. Moments of good do not end; moments of good encroach on evil and darkness. Good impacted on a soul is forever.

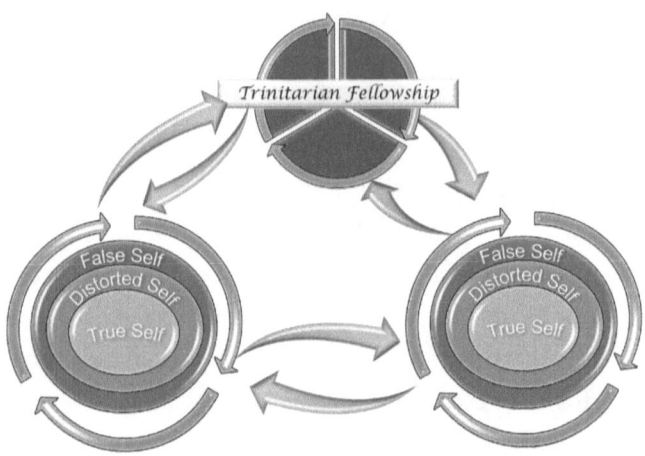

The other side of serving others is being served by others.

Ostensibly, it seems to be an easy task to receive from another. We all love to be served, but when it is free and done out of love, we get a bit twitchy. It messes with our innate concern about status. The welfare system is a good example. The only way people can continue to tolerate the ongoing assistance is to turn it inside out and make it what they deserve. Over time, it becomes a hardness that is not likely to change. This is then handed down to the next generation. Long term welfare can violate our sense of value, which is where we make most of our decisions; it is self-reinforcing.

Notice when Jesus washed the disciples' feet. At the time it was customary for servants to wash guests' feet before eating. To not wash feet would be like not offering to take a guest's winter coat, gloves, and hats and then inviting them to sit down to eat. The situation is just completely socially awkward and uncomfortable.

That tension was not lost on the disciples. The tension was about who would be greatest or least among them. A power struggle—who would submit to this very lowly task of washing feet. Jesus donned the towel of service.

Peter, visibly upset with the disruption of hierarchy, got a bit twitchy.

Jesus explained that this was the very nature of the kingdom relationship that he was being invited into. The nature of this relationship is love for another, service in action.

Peter, never one to disappoint, suggested that Jesus wash all of him.

The Kingdom of God is action with the greatest of governing principles: love God, love self, and love one another. The nature of kingdom love received is compelling. It must go out and must be shared. Service begets love begets service begets love.

MAKING IT PERSONAL

The classic disciplines, which are so important in our story as believers, are widely generic and have been engaged in by the many saints who have preceded us. In classic form, they are timeless, powerful, and important tools of transformation. Because the journey of transformation is unique to every soul called of God, the practice of disciplines can be tailored to each person's journey.

The discipline of making a salad

I love fresh vegetables. Again, I didn't think I was a good gardener. I disciplined myself to take care of that garden in the way we're supposed to take care of it. What got in the way was my distorted self. I disciplined myself to be in my true self and do the things I *can* do. I wanted to quit, because my distorted self kept telling me I couldn't do it. In the end, I had a salad. I learned something about God, that things have to die before they are resurrected. I learned carrots stay in the ground through the winter and will be there next spring. The earth is amazing; I got in relationship with the earth, which no one had taught me to do. I learned how little control I had, but I could still cooperate with the earth. I learned to manage my self and my inner critic, and learned discipline.

Gardening is slow, methodical. It's not going to work if you go out once a month and throw a lot of water on everything. I slowed down. Noticed my anxiety. "I'm too busy to water that garden." *No, you're not too busy. This is important.* I slowly walked out, around the house, enjoyed the walk, took my time, watered the garden, walked back. I learned to slow down and give grace to myself on days I didn't. I reveled in the miracle of the earth.

Discouraged and overwhelmed by our "lack of growth," we often make the mistake of biting off more than we can chew. We grab large topics such as humility and proceed to white-knuckle our way toward the accomplishment, only to be frustrated with our progress. White-knuckling is a sure sign that an activity is not being done in cooperation with the Holy Spirit. As the disciplines are practiced in small ways for a period of time, they become a habit and grow our kingdom nature. The disciplines are about getting the kingdom into us.

Some years ago, I did the classic parent activity of taking my children to piano lessons. One day, I asked if I could take the spot of one of my kids. I proceeded to take a couple piano lessons. Matt, our piano teacher, told me that playing the piano is about practice, practice, practice.

I sat down and said to Matt, "I can't do this."

He said, "Put your hands on the keyboard." And he started teaching me the notes. I was dealing with my distorted self: I can't do this. I'm not good enough. But before long, I was learning notes and playing music.

It is the practice that trains my finger to move. Playing piano is not about thinking about each note played and how to get my fingers there. It is about training my hands until it becomes automatic. I had to first make the choice to sit down in front of the piano and practice. In the practice, I was getting the piano into my hands. Christian development is often approached like sitting down at a piano and expecting a concerto to come from our fingertips. It does not work that way. The kingdom begins in the small. This truth reminds me of a mustard seed (Matthew 17:20).

One of my mustard seeds that needs to be watered is the practice of slowing down and being patient. While attending a program through Renovare Spiritual Formation Institute, we were invited to a monthly practice of getting in the slow lane, whether it was in traffic or the grocery line. The very concept hurt my brain. "Why? Why? Why would someone ever do that?" I attempted this extraordinarily bizarre behavior and was delightfully surprised. There are some beautiful church spires on the way to work that I have missed in the last decade.

I began to ponder what other things I might be missing. I began to take the time to water my plants. This pace of the kingdom began to invade my skin. Spiritually, I noticed small places that needed kingdom water: love and grace. I noticed that in the midst of my hurry or determination, I enjoyed taking time to put my agenda aside for the weightier matters of the law: justice, mercy, and faith, and matters of love: grace, time, hugs, and listening. The kingdom was becoming so real.

A personal relationship with God is just that personal. It is unique to you and Him. He has gifted us all differently and relates with us all differently. Of course, there are some general similarities. He invites us to pray—that is classic. How we do that is another matter—that is personal. Reading the Bible and Bible study is a common way of relating but, hey, how we do that can be as different as people are different. Some people hover, meditate, and soak on a small section of scripture for months and others read the entire Bible in a year. Disciplines are not a rigid "way of doing it right." Disciplines are simply ways of organizing our life so we can be present with God in order to cooperate with the Holy Spirit as we are being transformed.

CHAPTER 10

Commission

COMMISSION: RELATIONSHIP WITH ONE ANOTHER

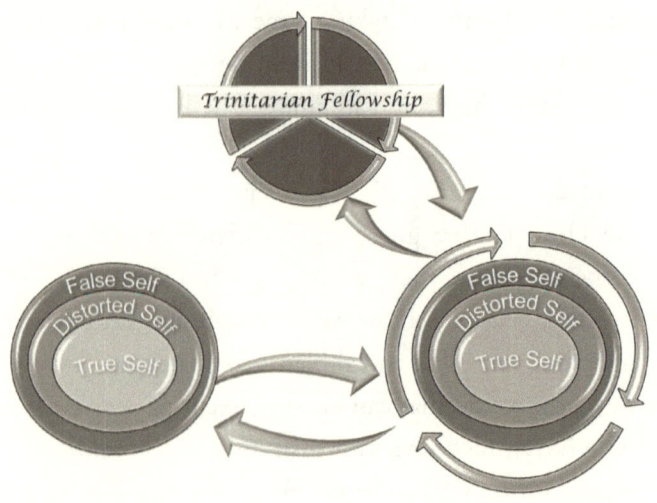

"The aim of God in human history is the creation of an all–inclusive community of loving persons, with Himself included in that community as its prime sustainer and most glorious inhabitant."
–Dallas Willard

Heaven's Envoys

L ives radiating the glorious presence and reality of God is the plan. While certainly God can and does work on a grand scale with big events—no mistaking the Red Sea situation or the tongues of fire event—God is also working in the seemingly mundane.

It is His presence with us as we interact with a person that we see every day and almost take for granted, don't even notice, or worse. It is here in the quiet, the unnoticeable, God is working—will you see it (Isaiah 43:19)? It is in you and me as we live our lives loving our neighbor (whom Dallas Willard defines as the person in front of you) at any given moment, in any given way, love emanating from the throne room reflected through you and me to others as we are in relationship with them.

Reflection of anything requires presence. The degree to which you are in the presence of anything is the degree to which you will reflect it. The more I am present with God the more I take on His character, demeanor, and essence. This is Christian spiritual formation. I then share it with whomever is in front of me.

I grew up in the South, the Kentucky, Tennessee, Missouri area. I have a southern accent. I have not lived there in well over twenty years, yet you can still hear it. I don't hear it and I make no effort at it, but I was immersed in it for twenty years. What might we be like when we are immersed in the environment of heaven? What accent might people hear if we live, eat, and breathe the kingdom? It matters and it shows. When we are immersed in that reality, we do not have to think about it or try to do it. It is just what is true. I do not ever think, "How would someone from the South say this?" Nor does someone immersed in the presence of God need to ask, "What Would Jesus Do?" Like my accent, it just comes out of where I have lived.

As love emanates from the throne to us, it flows out of our being. It is this love that overcomes evil.

The only way to overcome evil is to let it run itself to a standstill because it does not find the resistance it is looking for. Resistance merely creates further evil and adds fuel to the flames. But when evil meets no opposition and encounters no obstacle but only patient endurance, its sting is drawn, and at last it meets an opponent which is more than its match. Of course this can only happen when the last ounce of resistance is abandoned, and the renunciation of revenge is complete. Then evil cannot find its mark, it can breed no further evil, and is left barren. (Bonhoeffer, *The Cost of Discipleship*, 1959)

Service, love, kindness, peace, gentleness, self-control undergirded by the effectual work of grace in our lives as we interact with others' conveys or shadows forth the very essence of God to an evil world in much need of the throne's love. As we remain in the presence of God, our souls are transformed. Transformed souls then emanate the glory of the one whom they behold. We shadow forth!

The absolute brilliance of the plan is that our perfection is not required. It is His perfection that we don. Our perception of perfection is our expectation, and we have anchored it to the plan. Sadly, it is quite the heavy anchor and it has jammed some things up. In fact, I would suggest that it is our imperfection that is inviting to others and creates a sense of community. It is not our perfection but His perfect grace that is the draw.

And He has said to me, "My grace is sufficient for you, for power is perfected in weakness." Most gladly, therefore, I will rather boast about my weaknesses, so that the power of Christ may dwell in me. Therefore I am well content with weaknesses, with insults, with distresses, with persecutions, with difficulties, for Christ's sake; for when I am weak, then I am strong.

2 Corinthians 12:9–11

Shadowing Forth

Several churches I have been in lately display a written statement above the exiting doors that says, "You are entering the mission fields." Of course, we are. Not all of us are called to go to the farthest reaches of the earth. In fact, there is quite a bit to do right here—right in front of us. If we could allow God to be God and know that He is not only capable of carving out our life's path, but also capable of bringing people he chooses across that path, we might begin to see the kingdom grow right in front of us.

I know this is a hot topic for some, so let me be clear. I am not suggesting that we sit on our laurels and remain in our comfort zone. I am suggesting something far greater.

If we are cooperating with the Holy Spirit by staying in the presence of God, I am suggesting that God will put you exactly where He wants you. I would further suggest that you are strategically placed to reap the harvest that is in front of you. I continue in my boldness and suggest that if you feel called to leave your comfort zone and reach out to folks outside of where you are, that is God as well and He is moving your position.

God with Skin

Man was created a body, the Son of God appeared on earth in the body, He was raised in the body, in the sacrament the believer receives the Lord Christ in the body, and the resurrection of the dead will bring about the perfected fellowship of God's spiritual-physical creatures. The believer therefore lauds the Creator, the Redeemer, God, Father, Son and Holy Spirit, for the bodily presence of a brother. (Bonhoeffer, *Life Together*, 1954)

Understanding the seeable is challenging enough. Relating to the unseeable is a daunting task, which is made nearly impossible when we are in pain. When we are in pain (and most of us are in pain most of the time), understanding that a loving, compassionate, and caring God—who, by the way, is allowing this pain—is present with us in our pain makes absolutely no sense.

We can understand the warm hug of a friend. We can understand the shoulder of someone who hears our cry and carries our burden. We can understand the sympathy in the eyes of someone who cares. These relational responses we understand. Sometimes it is just too hard to understand an invisible God, even for the spiritually stout among us. We need skin.

Skin bridges the gap. The formidable love of a mother suggests a God who will never leave (Isaiah 49:15). The compassion of a friend who knows your sins and responds with compassion and understanding suggests a forgiving Father. The steadfastness of a friend in hard times suggests a God whose love endures. The friend who takes a day off work to sit with you in pain suggests a God who is intimate. The experience of another allows us to bridge a gap to the unseeable God who aches to be with us.

Truly His emissaries, we offer love and grace with "skin on" out of the deep love and grace we are submerged in. We offer this to the person in front of us. We offer forgiveness to the person who wronged us, knowing full well that justice will never be enacted. We offer grace in hard places where it is least expected. We offer our lives for others because we know we can barely comprehend the life given for us.

Interacting with one another—as "God with skin on" is relationship at its purest. It is this relationship through which God is building his kingdom one temple at a time. The challenge is to do relationship never perfectly but well. The greatest law—the driving principle of the Kingdom of God—is pure relationship, not perfect relationship.

Differentiation

Differentiation is a concept that has application across many disciplines of thought and practice—from metallurgy to mathematics to engineering. For our purposes, we will look at differentiation in the context of relationships, which has significant spiritual implications. Differentiation in the relationship context is an untangled awareness of the complex parts of the human condition and how to relate to those parts in ourselves and others independently while remaining connected.

> Differentiation of Self, or the ability to separate feelings and thoughts. Undifferentiated people cannot separate feelings and thoughts; when asked to think, they are flooded with feelings, and have difficulty thinking logically and basing their responses on that. Further, they have difficulty separating their own from other's feelings; they look to family to define how they think about issues, feel about people, and interpret their experiences.

> Differentiation is the process of freeing yourself from your family's processes to define yourself. This means being able to have different opinions and values than your family members but being able to stay emotionally connected to them. It means being able to calmly reflect on a conflicted interaction afterward, realizing your own role in it, and then choosing a different response for the future. (Bowenian Family Therapy, www.psychpage.com)

Relational Differentiation

Relationally we often struggle to not be tangled up in one another's emotional, psychological, and/or spiritual issues. These unhealthy entanglements have been sanitized by wrongly labeling the behavior as "family," "love," or "devotion." We all want and need to be connected; however, we can become overly connected to the point of harm. In the counseling business, we call this codependence or enmeshment.

We find enmeshment and codependency in larger groups as well. Connotatively the word *cult* is generally connected to religion, but we can find it in many other areas: higher educational institutions, governments, churches, service clubs, or corporations, any group where independent thought or action is not allowed and where members must conform to the acceptable standards and thoughts. These groups do not tolerate differentiation.

All systems (groups of people or things that are interconnected) have boundaries to one degree or another. These boundaries define the levels of closeness and flexibility. To the degree that these features are healthy or unhealthy defines our differentiation. Relationships without differentiation are unhealthy as the true self is subjected to others' definitions. For example, low levels of differentiation are present when

- young Sally plans on going into military service because her mother did and her father before her did despite her keen interest in another career. This decision is made because "we are a military family."
- in a church culture where intimate relationship cannot be sustained because of a differing opinion over music or Sunday school.
- a young person is hitting their mid-twenties has no interest in family but is consistently pressured to couple off and start creating offspring because that is what our good God commands. Apparently, we must procreate because it is one of the 11 commandments.

Low–level differentiation cannot tolerate differences in another, while healthy boundaries allow you to be you and me to be me and us to be in relationship with one another. In a healthy relationship we are clear that we are responsible *for* ourselves and responsible *to* each other.

Differentiation: Kingdom Implication

Grappling with the differentiation question "Who am I responsible for and who am I responsible to?" creates bright lines of distinction. Understanding these bright lines of distinction is crucial for kingdom impact. When pondering the heavy burden of having to save souls, consider the following:

Am I responsible for a soul to be saved or am I responsible to emanate the glory of God by way of loving the person in front of me, follow the leading of the Holy Spirit as He interacts with the person in front of me, and point the person in front of me back to Jesus?

Is this a situation where I am responsible for my sister in Christ changing her attitude, or am I responsible to my sister in Christ when I consider the part I am playing in the discord? Why am I so distressed? Is it really correction of my sister that is needed, or is it my need for justice? Is what must be applied here grace and compassion?

- Am I responsible for the cessation of my brother's sin or am I responsible to my brother to walk with him?
- Am I responsible for my neighbor to get to church or am I responsible to my neighbor to invite them?
- Am I responsible for the number of souls in the pews or is God?
- Am I responsible for the pleasing of the ears in the audience, or am I responsible to God to speak what might be unpleasant to hear?
- Am I responsible for how the church is run, or am I responsible for my role and responsible to the church to act in that role as I have been invited?
- Am I responsible for how the church dispenses funds allocated to them, or am I responsible to God to tithe?
- Am I responsible for the pastor getting corrective feedback?

It might be helpful to remember that Jesus leaned far more heavily on grace and compassion than judgment in responding to folks' sinning. Even Jesus knew that, in His current role, He was not responsible for the salvation of souls—that responsibility was the Father's (John 6:44).

Differentiation untangles our lives and puts us back in appropriate relationship with God, self, and one another. Differentiation simplifies the many challenges we face in all areas of our lives: family, marriage, church, God, work. I love my dear husband, but I am in no way responsible for him. I certainly attempted at times in our early years to be responsible for him (yeah, that did not work out very well). What John McMorris does is what John McMorris does. I do not stand for John; I cannot choose for him; I am not responsible for him. I can, however, stand with him. It is out of my responsibility to love a person I might choose to stand with them. Jesus died on that cross because He chose to out of love. It had to be His choice. He was responsible to us because of love as I am responsible to John because of love.

When we understand this differentiation, we set people free to be responsible for self—consequences and all. It is in this freedom that we set folks free to wrestle with God and not with us. It is not our scripture that we have to defend, it is God's to defend; our responsibility is to share.

When we understand differentiation, we set people free to be in relationship with God on their path, not our path. Differentiation is knowing the difference between me and you. I am not responsible for your actions in this life, but I am responsible for my actions toward you. I am your sister in Christ. I am bonded to you in Christ. I cannot save you. I can point you to Christ. I cannot keep you from sinning. I can shoulder your burden and hold your confession with compassion. I cannot accept the call of intimacy with Christ for you. I can share intimacy and safety with you and hold your pain and triumphs. I cannot walk your journey for you. I can walk with you. I am not Christ. I know where He is. When we can set people free to be in the hands of the living God, they are in the best position in life.

Years ago, I was whining to a friend that John wasn't going to church, and I was having to cajole him to do what I decided he needed to do. She stopped me mid-sentence and said, "Theressa, get out of God's way." I was dumbfounded, silent—not a place I get very often.

She nailed it. I had made myself a committee of one responsible for John's salvation. Everything changed in that moment. I began to pray from that day forward only for one thing for John—that God's will be done in his life. Seven months later, he quit his 401k, salaried, paid–vacation, with–benefits job and enrolled in seminary. I am responsible to John, and so I bring him before God's throne for His will to be done.

What would happen if we brought the people we loved before the throne of God for His will and not insist that this or that is done? What if we allowed God to be God and we stopped taking over His job?

I am not suggesting that we do not pray specifics for folks—in fact, Jesus encouraged that. I do, however, ask the question: might we ponder that God's will is perfect and put that in the mix of what we decide to pray about? When I do not pray for God's will but for my desires, it's fine. It is just where I am; He understands and wants to hear them. When my father was dying, I prayed for healing. That is where I was, and He certainly wants to hear our pleadings and desires. I offer this, however: might we give some brain cells to the work of differentiating between what our will is and what His might be?

The covenant I made with John decades ago now did not make me responsible for his choices; it made me responsible to him. I stand with him because I am responsible to him. In my responsibility to him I listen, share, reflect, pray for, encourage, confront, and discern with him, but, in the end, John McMorris is responsible for John McMorris. That doesn't sound very submissively lovingly sacrificially Christian-y, does it? That's right.

Saving Souls

For far too long, we have defined love in very unhealthy ways. When we believe or promote that we are supposed to be out there "saving souls" we suggest that we are God (John 6:44). Nowhere in scripture does it suggest that we can save anything—not even ourselves. How could we save others? This distinction is important: if we are saving souls, we are saving unto ourselves. Most likely, we are just getting people to copy us, making disciples of ourselves. This was not the admonition of Jesus.

If we could pull it off, we would bring folks to the altar kicking and screaming and say the words for them. We can't do that, so we cajole, manipulate, browbeat, harass, condemn, judge, shame, and guilt one another because we think we know what is best for folks. Are we selling God or a car? What would it look like not to do that? What if we simply cooperated with the leading of the Holy Spirit when we are with folks and go as far as we are invited to go?

The answer to every person's query about God is not to march them to the altar. Just answer the question and see what God does with it. Marching folks to the altar, ignoring their resistance or questions, is about our anxiety about needing to save a soul. Our job is not to save souls; it is to be in relationship with folks with "skin on" as God is working in their lives. We are invited to be present with God as He is present in others' lives. We are invited to point folks to Jesus.

I was sitting with someone one time who was witnessing to someone. The believer told the person to get a booklet from a certain church and read it next to the Bible. I almost jumped out of my skin. When that person left and I only had a few moments, I looked at the dazed woman and said, "Just read the Bible. You might start in the Gospels; the book of John is a good read." The good-hearted believer was not pointing to Jesus; he was pointing to a church and its doctrine.

A Differentiated Jesus

Psychology has a sordid history with the church for good reason; however, I would suggest that Jesus was not only differentiated, but He was the most excellent of psychology professors. The current practice of healthy psychological discovery has only ever uncovered the truth about the creation of mankind, how we work with ourselves, and how we work with others. We have great Christian minds who uncover and work brilliantly hard at understanding our relationship with God.

Jesus was constantly teaching the people around Him about good and healthy boundaries. James and John, wanting to be in the power position, were told to be more thoughtful about what they asked, and that the decision was not Jesus' to make. Jesus constantly challenged people to think properly and to think through distortions. He called attention to the Pharisees revealing that they were more concerned about microscopic self-righteous tithing than with the matters at the core of God's concern: justice, mercy, and faith.

Differentiated, He let people make the decisions that they were going to make and never got tugged to manipulate them to make the right one. When dealing with the rich young ruler, it must have been so very hard to see him make the decision to value his riches over relationship. When Judas was headed toward finishing the transaction to betray Him, He said, "What you are about to do, do quickly." Jesus outed the Pharisees in Luke 16:16–31. They made excuses, but in the end, they were responsible for themselves and what they knew. He outright told them that they knew the truth and that they were what we call in the business rationalizing (verse 15). Rationalizing only works for a time because in the end, consequences are consequences.

Differentiation is not an easy process and at first blush can look unloving, but if we go beneath the surface, we begin to see that at its heart is love and respect. To be undifferentiated is to usurp the authority in a person's life and remove consequences. If my child chooses to not pay their cell phone bill and I pay it for them, I have taken their free will. Their free will was to not pay the phone bill knowing the consequences. For them not to experience the consequences is to steal their consequences. Free will cannot be separated from its outcome, or it is enslavement.

It must have been hard for Jesus to watch Judas go. I am sure there was part of Jesus that wanted to plead with the rich young ruler not to go. Differentiation is letting love do its great work. The parable of the prodigal son describes a loving, generous father who loved his son very much and knew he needed to let him go. The wise father knew what his son was going to do and that he could not control his path. How hard would that have been to let his son go, knowing what he was seeking and what was in his heart? The son had to come to his senses (Luke 15:17) so that he could see his consequences and what love held for him. Love always must remain free.

Kingdom love is one soul serving another soul while pointing to Jesus, who points to the Father, who sends the Holy Spirit. One soul loving another soul in service and then letting the person do what they will with the service. The love of the kingdom is unabashedly given to anyone who believes, while never requiring an outcome. Of course, we desire that all would be saved (so does He), but the outcome is not up to us. It is free will. If someone chooses not to be with God, then that in the end is free will and the consequences of that free will. Let us love each other as we each individually stay in God's loving embrace. Let us trust that kingdom love will do its great work.

Spiritual Differentiation

Differentiation is a word employed in many different contexts inclusive of math, biology, science, diagnosis, and relationships. Differentiation is the process of identifying the differences between objects, concepts, entities, etc. Differentiation is very much a clarifying and orientating process. If you have ever been around young people in love, you get the sense that somehow their bodies became fused because there is rarely any separation. His thoughts are her thoughts. Her dreams are his dreams. This is the reason marriage counselors rarely get to do any pre-marital counseling. Because there are no problems. There is perfect union! They are already one! This we might be able to call "undifferentiated."

Differentiation allows us to see that God is not creating automa-tons. He does not need to make another Abby or Omar; he already has one of each. God is not Xerox. He is a wild untamable God inviting you to do a very scary thing—be free in Him. The invitation is to engage in this unfathomable journey designed for such a time as this.

God is not building a kingdom of cookie–cutter temples for the Holy Spirit; He is creating unique individuals who dare to carve out with him a path not yet paved. This is a God who made kangaroos and galaxies and quarks and flamingos and you. He does not tend to be bor-ing and repetitive. . . again, we do that.

Spiritual differentiation is when we understand someone else's rela-tionship with God to be their own and let it stand independently of us while in relationship to us. Spiritual differentiation is the knowledge and action of pointing not to ourselves but to God. Spiritual differentiation is when we can know the difference between our self, one another, and God. He is not who we make Him to be but who He has defined Him-self to be. He has set us free to choose to be in relationship with Him or not. As we stay in the presence of the Almighty, we cannot but point to Him. He is the compelling power source of this kingdom.

The Blueprint

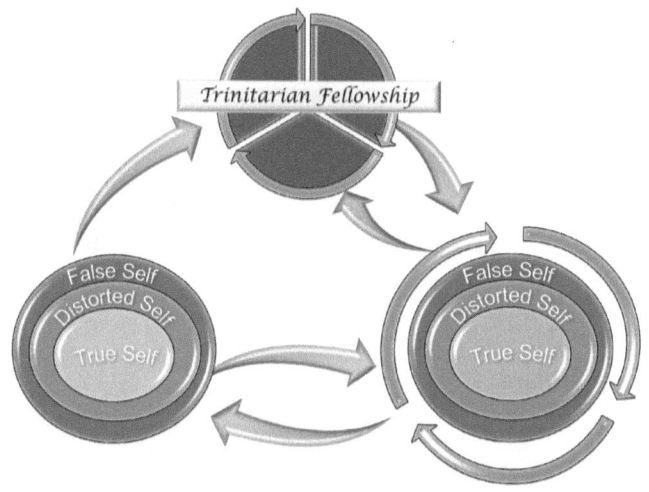

Love magnetically pulls us toward God and then it must undeniably billow out to the world. This is the nature of love. I quoted this before but want to reflect on it again.

"He is Three Persons, but One God. . . One Infinite Love in three subsistent relations. . . In the Father the infinite love of God is always beginning and in the Son it is always full and in the Holy Spirit it is perfect and it is renewed and never ceases to rest in its everlasting source. But if you follow Love forward and backward from Person to Person, you can never track it to a stop, you can never corner it and hold it down and fix it to one of the Persons as if He could appropriate to Himself the fruit of the love of the others. For the One Love of the Three Persons is an infinitely rich giving of Itself which never ends and is never taken, but is always perfectly given, only received in order to be perfectly shared" (Merton, *Seeds of Contemplation*, p. 68).

"Love of the Three. . . is always perfectly given, only received in order to be perfectly shared." It's compelling; its nature is that it must be given again. Love does not often need to be taught to new parents; no need to tell a mom to care for her child—love compels her. The same is true for living in the kingdom; kingdom living is self-replicating and compelling. As we live our lives out of kingdom living, others are drawn, we point back to Jesus, and the beckoning begins anew. Just as the Father points to the Son, the Son points to the Father, and the Holy Spirit does what the Father says, we point to the center of all relationships—Jesus.

The goal is set.

"The aim of God in human history is the creation of an all–inclusive community of loving persons, with Himself included in that community as its prime sustainer and most glorious inhabitant."
–Dallas Willard

The invitation is given.

"I am with you; will you be with me?" –Richard Foster

Will you enter into relationship?

- Relationship with 'Elohiym, which by virtue of His mere presence will spiritually transform you into the likeness of Jesus Christ and mature you into who you were rightly designed to be before the whisper?
- Relationship with yourself where you can know and embrace your true self?
- Relationship with one another where your true transformed self emanates the glorious presence of God to your community as all partake in the *yada* nature of the Trinity?

The nature of the kingdom is relational. Relationship is all there is. There is nothing else.

Characteristics of the False, Distorted, and True Self

	Source of Knowledge	Characteristics	Orientation
False Self	Messages from distorted self	Defends Protects Serves Manipulates Justifies Minimizes Excuses	Self-focused Other person-centered At the service of the distorted self
Distorted Self	Distorted truths, mistruths, misconceptions, lies, condemnations, judgments, incorrect conclusions	Shame Guilt Fearfulness Anxiousness Judgement Condemnation	Measured by what others think (other person-centered) Focused on relief of real or anticipated pain (self-focused) Driven to relieve pain Driven to be "good enough"
True Self	Truth: strengths and challenges	Safe Non-anxious Accepting of pain Sufficient Objective Compassionate Curious Reflective Truth-seeking	Engaged in process Works out of strengths Works at challenges Measured by progress only of self not others (centered in self) Concerned about how to serve and help others (other person-focused)

Beumer, Jurjen. (1998). *Henri Nouwen: A Restless Seeking for God.* New York: The Crossroad Publishing Company.

Bonhoeffer, Dietrich (1959). *The Cost of Discipleship.* New York: Touchstone

Bonhoeffer, Dietrich (1954). *Life Together: The Classic Exploration of Christian Community.* New York: HarperCollins.

Bowen Family Therapy – Psych Page, (http://www.psychpage.com/learning/library/counseling/bowen.html.

Carter, John D., Narramore, S. Bruce (1979). *The Integration of Psychology and Theology. An Introduction.* Grand Rapids: The Zondervan Corporation.

Coursey, Chris M., (2016). *Transforming Fellowship: 19 Brain Skills That Build Joyful Community.* East Peoria: Shepherds House.

Foster, Richard, J. (2009-03-17). *Celebration of Discipline.* San Francisco: HarperCollins. [Kindle Edition].

Foster, Richard J. (2009-10-13). *Life with God: Reading the Bible for Spiritual Transformation.* HarperCollins. [Kindle Edition].

Foster, Richard J. (1992). *PRAYER: Finding the Hearts True Home.* New York: HarperCollins. [Kindle Edition].

Foster, Richard J. (2010-10-12). *Streams of Living Water: Celebrating the Great Traditions of Christ.* HarperCollins. [Kindle Edition].

Gesenius Lexicon (www.blueletterbible.org).

Johnson, Darrell, (2015). Entering the Trinity, Living in the Circle of "US." *Conversations, 13(1), 15–18.*

Kelly, Thomas R. (1941). *A Testament of Devotion.* New York, NY: HarperCollins.

Lawrence, Brother. (2008). *The Collected Works of Brother Lawrence The Practice of the Presence of God.* [Kindle Edition].

Merton, Thomas. (2003). *The Inner Experience: Notes on Contemplation.* New York: HarperCollins.

Merton, Thomas. (1949). *Seeds of Contemplation* (New York: New Directions Books).

Nouwen, Henri J. M. (2010). *Spiritual Formation: Following the Movements of the Spirit.* HarperCollins e-books.

Nouwen, Henri J. M., Christensen, Michael, J., Laird, Rebecca J. (2006) *Spiritual Direction: Wisdom for the Long Walk of Faith.* New York: HarperCollins.

Roxburgh, Alan J. and Fred Romanuk. (2020). *The Missional Leader: Equipping Your Church to Reach a Changing World.* Minneapolis: Fortress Press.

St. Nikodimos of the Holy Mountain, St. Makarios of Corinth. (1979). *The Philokalia: The Complete Text.* New York: Faber and Faber, Inc.

Strong's Concordance (www.blueletterbible.org).

Tozer, A.W. *The Dwelling Place of God.* [Kindle Edition].

Wilhoit, James C. (2008). *Spiritual Formation as if the Church Mattered: Growing in Christ through Community.* Grand Rapids: Baker Academic.

Willard, Dallas, (1997). *The Divine Conspiracy: Recovering Our Hidden Life in God.* San Francisco: HarperCollins [Kindle Edition].

Willard, Dallas (2011). *Renovation of the Heart: Putting on the Character of Christ with Bonus Content (Designed for Influence).* Colorado Springs: NavPress [Kindle Edition].

Willard, Dallas (2006). *The Great Omission: Reclaiming Jesus' Essential Teaching on Discipleship.* San Francisco: HarperCollins [Kindle Edition].

Willard, Dallas (2009-02-06). *The Spirit of the Disciplines: Understanding How God Changes Lives.* San Francisco: HarperCollins. [Kindle Edition].

Theressa McMorris is a licensed Marriage and Family Therapist, Spiritual Formation Director, author, speaker, doctoral student, AAMFT Approved Supervisor, church consultant, and business owner of one of the largest sole MFT practices in New York state founded on kingdom principles. Working in upstate New York for eighteen years, Theressa is driven by a passion for promoting healthy relationship with God, self, and one another. She has a simple message. The Kingdom of God is now and is intended to be manifested in each of our lives as a beacon of light wherever we have been planted. Theressa attempts to live this out and invites others to join the journey and the conversation.

Theressa is a devoted follower of Christ, mother of three loves, and wife of a wonderful man for twenty-seven years. She loves coffee, learning, fresh food, feeding people, and laughing. When not tackling homework, she reads about the early church, spiritual formation, and the many different faith traditions. Theressa was raised in the small rural town of Metropolis, Illinois, which happens to be the hometown of Superman. She has lived in Texas, California, and Tennessee but has landed in Syracuse, New York, home of college basketball, over 100 inches of snow yearly, amazing apples, and four beautiful seasons.

www.ingramcontent.com/pod-product-compliance
Lightning Source LLC
Chambersburg PA
CBHW031414120626
46545CB00006B/2135